We Met Morris:

Interviews with
William Morris,
1885-96

In Memory of Nicholas Salmon (1957–2002).

We Met Morris:
Interviews with William Morris, 1885-96

edited by
Tony Pinkney

Spire Books Ltd
in association with the
William Morris Society

Contents

Introduction

This book gathers together thirteen interviews with William Morris which appeared in newspapers or journals between 1885 and 1896, the year of his death. The idea of such a volume was first mooted by Nicholas Salmon, author of *The William Morris Chronology* and editor of two major collections of Morris's political journalism, who, however, sadly did not live to bring it to fruition. He had transcribed six of these interviews before his premature death at the age of forty-four in 2002 and had prepared a rough draft introduction. I have incorporated some material and emphases from that draft in my own introduction where appropriate, and this volume is accordingly dedicated to Nick. It can serve as an interim tribute until we finally get that volume of his collected essays on Morris which will clearly establish him as the leading Morris scholar of his generation.[1]

Taken as a whole, the thirteen interviews collected here give us a vivid sense of Morris as he appeared to his contemporaries: of his range of activities and preoccupations, his places of work and leisure, his clothes, gestures, moods and phrases. The interviewers often invite Morris to expound his views on socialism, arts and crafts, aesthetics, architecture, or printing, and he obliges fluently, giving us some memorable formulations of Morrisian doctrine in these pages. But they also frequently challenge him, prompting new efforts of definition on his part and sometimes striking extensions of his thought too. Morris proves in these interviews to be as restless intellectually as he often is physically, constantly pressing forward into new fields of artistic endeavour, and always relating these to the wider politics of his society.

In her *William Morris: A Life for our Time* Fiona MacCarthy notes that as early as 1870 Morris 'had become a public figure', as evidenced by 'the sequence of photographs and portraits to which [he] was submitting himself, much against his will'.[2] With the interviews gathered here, from 1885 onwards, we clearly pass into another, more intensive phase of Morris's emergence as a Victorian celebrity, in which it is not simply his image but his opinions which are increasingly valued by the press. The newspaper interview was in fact an invention of the mid-Victorian period. As Lucy Brown notes, in her *Victorian News and Newspapers*, 'the *Oxford Dictionary* gives the earliest reference to the word interview, in the press sense, as taking place in 1867'. And it has been argued that W.T. Stead, editor of the *Pall Mall Gazette* (from which two interviews with Morris feature here), was the inventor of the 'at home' style of interview which dominates this volume.[3]

Why, then, was Morris considered so interview-worthy by his contemporaries? The answer emerges in the titles to some of the pieces in this collection: 'The Poet and the Police', 'Poet as Printer', 'A Socialist Poet on Bombs and Anarchism'. Morris first emerged as 'the Poet' with the enormous success of *The Earthly Paradise* as it appeared in four volumes between 1868 and 1870. Thereafter the middle-class public saw him as a worthy successor in the Romantic lineage of Keats and Tennyson, and the fact that a poet in this mould – the 'idle singer of an empty day', as the Apology to *The Earthly Paradise* famously puts it – could simultaneously be a highly successful craftsman-designer and above all, from 1883, a revolutionary socialist seems to have been a shock that Morris's middle-class contemporaries never quite got over and yet remained deeply fascinated by. 'The Poet and the Police': how *could* those two terms have anything to do with each other? How could the rarefied upper reaches of literature possibly have anything to do with the police harassment of political street meetings in the mid-1880s? Yet, in the burly person of Morris, they palpably and undeniably did.

It is, then, this hybrid identity – Poet as Printer, Poet as Socialist – that so bemuses and intrigues many of his interviewers. One of them even refers to Morris as 'the Poet' (capital P) throughout, as if the reporter is absolutely unable to escape from this constricting definition of his interviewee. This generic bafflement – what manner of man am I dealing with here? – sometimes transfers itself onto Morris's physical surroundings, as with the *Clarion* interviewer who wanders disconsolately around Hammersmith looking for Kelmscott House, which seems almost wilfully to elude him. Indeed, as the series of interviews progresses, we get a sense of Kelmscott House, Morris's London dwelling from November 1878 to his death in October 1896, as a resonant symbolic location, charged with the full mystery and diversity of his preoccupations. True, there are glimpses here of Morris in other locales – at his Merton Abbey works, or parked sturdily in front of one of his own tapestries at the 1893 Arts and Crafts exhibition at London's New Gallery. But it is clearly Kelmscott House which dominates the collective imagination of his interviewers. The contrast of its stolid bourgeois exterior and its interior of Morrisian decoration, assorted art treasures and, increasingly in later years, ancient books and manuscripts, articulates in the reporters' minds something of the paradox, the schizophrenia even, which they tend to see in the man himself. How, after all, can one place be both a medieval time-capsule and, as the second *Pall Mall Gazette* visitor terms it, 'the centre of Socialism'? This issue, of the relation between Morris's medievalism and his socialism, is indeed crucial to any full assessment of his work, and I shall return to it below.

Three major areas of concern emerge in the interviews

collected here: Morris's politics, his views of crafts in general and tapestry in particular, and the Kelmscott Press and its books. The aim of this introduction is to establish a general context for each of these, which will then be complemented by more detailed headnotes and footnotes for each of the texts which follow.

Morris's arrival at revolutionary socialism in 1883 was the endpoint of an accelerating process of cultural and political radicalisation since the mid-1870s. In 1876 he had become treasurer of the Eastern Question Association, which campaigned against the Disraeli government's threat to go to war with Russia on behalf of the Turks, whose brutal massacres in Bulgaria were fresh in the public mind. But Morris's full emergence into public life dates from 1877, when he founded the Society for the Protection of Ancient Buildings, for which he was a formidable campaigner for much of the rest of his life, and gave his first public lecture, on 'The Decorative Arts', in London. His growing dissatisfaction with Liberal policies on Egypt and Ireland after Gladstone's return to power in 1880 pushed him further and further to the left, to the point where he joined H.M. Hyndman's Democratic Federation early in 1883. Hyndman's organisation shortly thereafter changed its name to Social Democratic Federation (SDF), thereby declaring its Marxist political allegiances, and, in an important symbolic gesture, Morris himself boldly announced his revolutionary socialism in a lecture on 'Art under Plutocracy' in Oxford, his old university, in November 1883.

The first interview here, 'A Talk with William Morris on Socialism', catches Morris at a crucial transitional moment in his career as revolutionary. His authority as a Marxist intellectual is already impressive, and he clearly has a wide knowledge of the European socialist movement. Morris's socialism is still, even today, sometimes presented as insular and peculiarly 'English'. But there is nothing parochial about the figure we see in action here. He has, as the interviewer notes with awe, 'the literature of Socialism at his finger-ends' and can discourse learnedly on why the German Marxist movement has acquired its distinctively scientific and centralist cast.

But in the British movement itself all is not well. The *Daily News* interviewer has heard rumours of a 'schism' in the SDF, and Morris sets out the reasons why he and others have felt compelled to break away from Hyndman and set up the Socialist League and its new paper, *Commonweal*, whose first issue appeared in February 1885. *Commonweal* was from the start impressively international, in line with the vision of socialism Morris sets out in this text; one of its main features was a 'record of the International Movement', edited by Karl Marx's daughter, Eleanor Marx Aveling. But it was also committed, as Morris notes here, to 'purist doctrines of Socialism', and this notion of ideological 'purity' and its practical implications is worth probing further.

Much of the dispute within the SDF had been about Hyndman's autocratic and jingoist tendencies. A 'purist' view of socialism partly means getting rid of all that, of disciplining one's personal and national vanity in the name of a genuinely collective and cosmopolitan cause. But the term also has a further meaning for Morris and bears upon practical socialist tactics as well as ethics. How, in a parliamentary democracy like Britain, should the emerging socialist movement proceed, how should it envisage the road to power? One very ready answer was, of course, to get socialists elected to Parliament in order to argue the cause there and press for practical measures to benefit the working class. Morris, however, was profoundly opposed to this parliamentary focus, which he saw as a distraction from the full, revolutionary aims of socialism. His 'purist' vision of the road forward, what he himself termed his 'policy of abstention', was essentially educational and organisational.[4] One must 'make socialists', in his famous slogan, slowly build a great movement outside Parliament dedicated to the eventual overthrow of capitalism. It isn't until the early 1890s, as we see in his later interview with *Justice*, that Morris shifts from this position and reassesses the strategic importance of Parliament for socialism.

Almost at the very moment of its emergence, then, English socialism had fissured down the middle. But in the short term there was much that the Socialist League and the SDF could agree and act jointly upon. This was particularly the case through 1885, when the British police mounted a sustained campaign of harassment of socialist open-air meetings. It was clearly incumbent upon all socialists, and radicals more generally, to defend the rights of free association and free speech. The second political interview in this sequence, with the *Pall Mall Gazette*, catches Morris at precisely this moment of his early socialist career, at the point where his own appearance in the dock in September 1885 had made him something of a media celebrity (or notoriety) in the middle-class press.

The *Justice* interview of 1894 shows us Morris at a later moment of crisis for the socialist movement, where the difficulty is not just police harassment from without but turmoil within the wider revolutionary movement itself. Morris had left the Socialist League in 1890 after it had succumbed to anarchist influence, and in response to the international anarchist bombing campaign of the early 1890s he forcefully expresses his opinions about such attacks in this text. He sees them as both criminal and counter-productive, sketches in contrast what he believes to be the correct contemporary tactics of socialists, and in so doing importantly shifts from the 'purism' of his earlier stance. Morris does here at last acknowledge a role for Parliament, and socialist representation in Parliament, in the struggle for social transformation; but this does not mean that he has simply collapsed back into the reformism and gradualism of the Fabian socialists of his day. Parliament must be used, crucially, to 'legalise revolt'. Morris thereby achieves a dialectical synthesis of the two 'extreme' options represented by the anarchists and the Fabians. The anarchists are right that violence will be necessary to transform society root and branch; the ruling class is unlikely to surrender its privileges without a vicious last–ditch struggle. But they are wrong in thinking that such violence can begin right here and now; such gestures are simply individual acts of terrorism, not the disciplined physical force of a great movement of collective change. The Fabians, on the other hand, are right that gaining influence in Parliament is important, but they are wrong in seeing this as an end in itself, as a way of gradually 'permeating' the old society and pushing reforms through stage by stage. Socialist representation in Parliament is, for Morris, still part of a revolutionary struggle. It undermines the ruling-class legitimacy of the use of force as the struggle approaches its decisive stage and thus hopefully makes proletarian 'force … much less likely to be necessary and much more likely to be successful'.

Perhaps the most spirited of the political interviews – indeed, perhaps of all the interviews gathered here – is that by Sarah Tooley on women's issues. Tooley herself is very aware of walking through the landscapes of Morris's *News from Nowhere* as she approaches his Hammersmith home, and as we read her text it is indeed as if the pages of Morris's utopia have opened and its most vigorous character, Ellen, has emerged to challenge her creator about women's rights in his own time. From our standpoint, Morris comes as across as decidedly ambivalent here. He certainly wants to see all the legal, political and moral inequalities under which women suffer in the 1890s removed. On the other hand, deep-seated Victorian assumptions about sexual and gender difference continue to constrain his thought: women are physically weaker than men, which means they cannot do certain kinds of craft work in particular, and he seems even to imply that women are intellectually feebler than men, with impressive practical organisational abilities but no real artistic talent 'up to the high-level mark'. Housekeeping turns out to be what, in Morris's view, women are best suited for, as indeed appears to be the case in the early Hammersmith Guest House chapters in his *News from Nowhere*.

One has to admire Sarah Tooley's pluck here as she continues to argue the feminist case against her august interviewee. As the conversation proceeds Morris's conservative prejudices seem to become more entrenched, and his tone becomes on occasion somewhat high-handed, even browbeating. Yet the reporter remains undaunted, not only not giving in but actually scoring some sharp polemical points against her famous adversary ('The advanced woman does not despise house-keeping, Mr. Morris; she only brings brain to it'). But given her strong reminiscences of *News from Nowhere* as she approaches Kelmscott House, it is surprising that Tooley does not invoke Morris's own utopia against him in the course of this dispute. For while the women in Hammersmith Guest House may indeed be limited to housekeeping, later in the text, as William Guest travels up the Thames to Kelmscott Manor, we come across Philippa the carver, who with her mallet and chisel energetically leads a team who are building a new house. No nonsense there about women not having the strength to be effective craft workers! And even more importantly we meet Ellen herself, certainly the most vivid and vigorous character in the book, physically athletic but proof too that women's intellectual abilities are indeed up to the high-level mark. Such impressive female figures have their counterparts in Morris's late prose romances too, above all in Birdalone in *The Water of the Wondrous Isles*. 'Never trust the artist; trust the tale', D.H. Lawrence once remarked; and there are times when Morris's literary texts may be better guides than his public pronouncements.

The second main area of concern in this volume is Morris's practice of the crafts in general and of tapestry in particular. It is a story often told how his inability to find satisfactory furniture and domestic items for the Red House which Philip Webb had built for him in 1859-60 prompted him to start a firm to manufacture such articles, and Morris, Marshall, Faulkner & Co. was accordingly established in April 1861 (though in actual fact Morris's decorative interests predated Red House by several years). The Firm produced embroideries, table glass, stained glass, furniture, painted tiles, jewellery, and in later years chintzes, carpets and of course the wall-papers for which Morris is still so famous. In attempting to break down the sharp division between designer and artisan which, following John Ruskin, he regarded as having been so disastrous for the English decorative arts, Morris sought to master the practical processes of the various media for which he designed, often returning to abandoned traditional techniques as he did so. At war with an 'age of shoddy', he was also devoted, as the *Clarion* reporter notes below, to the use of the most natural and best quality materials he could lay his hands upon. No stone was to be left unturned in the quest for what the Firm's first advertising circular called 'art beauty' in the objects of everyday life. By the late 1870s Morris's attention was turning to yet another new venture in the field of the decorative arts, as he set up a loom in his bedroom at Kelmscott House and began on 10th May 1879 to weave his *Acanthus and Vine* tapestry. These early experiments were relatively smallscale, and it was not until Morris transferred his works to Merton Abbey in 1881 that he was in a position to produce the truly spectacular tapestries designed by Edward Burne-Jones which so impress the *Daily Chronicle* and *Studio* interviewers.

What was the 'art beauty' to which Morris's decorative efforts were devoted, in tapestry and in the other crafts? The question is raised in two of the later interviews in this collection. 'Do People Appreciate the Beautiful?' asks the *Cassell's Saturday Journal* reporter, affording Morris an opportunity to fulminate against contemporary architectural developments, from country cottages to recent work on Westminster Abbey. The reporter makes a mild effort to resist the tirade he has unleashed, wondering if there might not be merit in at least some contemporary buildings (unfortunately he does not specify which he has in mind). But Morris's dominant personality clearly wins this exchange hands down.

Matters are not so clearcut in the *Daily Chronicle* interview on 'Art, Craft, and Life'. The interviewer is a more robust intellectual presence than his *Cassell's* counterpart, and the discussion focuses on beauty in tapestry rather than architecture, where Morris is perhaps on weaker ground. How can it possibly be appropriate, the reporter asks Morris, for a Victorian artist to produce these spectacular Holy Grail tapestries? For medieval artists such topics were part of a living belief system, but for us they merely belong to an exploded, long-past mythology. Why can we not find beauty in the struggles and belief systems of our own day? Morris replies forcefully, and the reader will have to decide for him or herself how persuasive his extended defence of his tapestry, and the concept of beauty it embodies, actually is. In my view, the reporter has certainly touched a key issue here (it will come up again in relation to the Kelmscott Press books): how does one draw the line between a medievalism that is energising and one that is merely nostalgic? By reminding us that life and art were once radically different, medievalism may alert us to the possibility that they could be so again, beyond capitalism; in this case it invigorates us in the present, stirs us towards an active and different future. But medievalism can equally become a wistful hankering back to the world of romance, to paradise lost or a happy Hobbitland rather than the paradise regained of socialist struggle. Perhaps, as a very rough rule of thumb, Morrisian medievalism tends towards the energising, as in *A Dream of John Ball*, his prose romance of the Peasants' Revolt of 1381, while Burne-Joncsian medievalism, as in the Holy Grail tapestries, tends towards the wistful.

The third major area of Morris's work to be picked up in these interviews is printing and book design, to which no less than four of them are dedicated. 'The Kelmscott Press was operated in the glare of publicity', writes its best recent historian, William S. Peterson, and a diary entry for 22nd May 1895 by its secretary, Sydney Cockerell, reveals just how intensive this exposure could be: 'press invaded in the af[ternoo]n by 60 members of the Librarians' Association. Went off all right however'.[5] The *Pall Mall Gazette*, interviewing Morris about the Kelmscott Press in November 1891, was quick off the mark here, since the Press had only issued its first book, Morris's own *The Story of the Glittering Plain*, in May of that year (followed in October by *Poems by the Way*, which is the focus of the interview). Yet Morris's interest in the book arts and fine printing can be traced back many years before this. Its starting point was his enthusiasm for the illuminated manuscripts in the Bodleian Library during his student days at Oxford. It emerged again in his desire to produce an illustrated version of *The Earthly Paradise* with Burne-Jones, that ambitious but unsuccessful project which Joseph Dunlap memorably termed 'The Book That Never Was'.[6] It then came through in a more sustained way in his experiments with calligraphy and illumination in the early 1870s, which produced such exquisite masterpieces as the *Book of Verse* he wrote out for Georgiana Burne-Jones. And it began to come to a focus with the keen interest Morris took in the printing of his *The House of the Wolfings* and *The Roots of the Mountains* at the Chiswick Press in the late 1880s.

At Emery Walker's lecture on 'Letter Press Printing' at the Arts and Crafts exhibition in November 1888 Morris reached the point of no return. This occasion it was, his daughter May asserted, which determined him to found the Kelmscott Press. Much careful research and experiment with typography, paper and ink followed before the first books rolled off the Press in 1891. Morris gives an energetic exposition of the principles of the Kelmscott Press in the interviews on this topic, and a vivid evocation of books already published and of his plans for the future. But more general and probing topics are raised here too. How, after all, do these lavishly decorated, beautifully produced and accordingly extremely expensive books relate to Morris's principles as a socialist? Hand-produced in natural materials, the Kelmscott books are indeed a delight to handle, now as then; but they were only affordable to the wealthy middle class in Morris's own time and, having become collectors' items subsequently, to the very wealthy indeed today. Once again, as with the Holy Grail tapestries, the issue of medievalism comes to the fore. Is the Kelmscott Press, as some later commentators have claimed, the place where even Morris's medievalism becomes nostalgic, a self-indulgent withdrawal from the admirable political engagement of earlier years?

Morris's pleasure in his creations, often vividly expressed in these interviews, especially in that with *Bookselling*, is infectious, but only sharpens rather than resolves the difficulty here. However, the shape of an answer emerges when the *Pall Mall Gazette* reporter pushes Morris into a vision of how his beloved early books and manuscripts might circulate in an achieved socialist society. With this sudden utopian vista of 'a public library at each street corner' Morris almost writes for us a new chapter of his *News from Nowhere,* which has sometimes been criticised for giving books and reading, even intellectual life in general, too small a role in its post-revolutionary vision (the 'Art, Craft, and Life' interview adds to this a glimpse of the guild system that may support artists and writers in utopia). Old Hammond argues in *News from Nowhere* that a society freed from the insane competitive pressures of the capitalist world-market will at last have space and leisure to decide how it wants to educate its children and produce its everyday wares. It can devote as much time and care as it wishes to these central human activities, which will no doubt include the printing of beautiful books. We can therefore expect the latter to be as gorgeously decorated in a socialist utopia as that extraordinary pipe William Guest picks up in the Piccadilly market in *News from Nowhere* itself. From this standpoint, then, the Kelmscott Press books, however expensive and restricted in social circulation in their own day, are not evidences of medievalist nostalgia and political withdrawal, but are rather time-travellers from some far future we can as yet barely imagine, showing how lovingly artefacts might be crafted in the socialist world that is to come. This is an argument which we can generalise to all the products of Morris and Co, not just to the Kelmscott books of his later years.

What did Morris himself make of the flurry of media attention he was receiving in the late 1880s and 1890s? What, in particular, did he make of the interviews which are gathered in this volume? We get a glimpse of his response in the later reflections of Sarah Tooley on 'Interviewing as Women's Work'. She recalls here that she had visited Morris at Kelmscott House for a second time, just before his death in 1896, for another interview. In the course of so doing, she had shown him the text of her *Woman's Signal* interview of 1894:

> Running his eye down the page, he caught sight of my little bit of personal description. He pretended to be highly indignant, but smiled all the same. 'Now if you write another interview with me,' he said, 'you must leave my clothes alone. None of that *delicate tracery and lacework*, you know! People don't want to hear about my clothes!' I could not help laughing, and he laughed too, with that comical twinkle of his, as he showed me out. I felt too sorry for his evident suffering to take advantage of his invitation to call again, and shortly afterwards he died.[7]

One appreciates Morris's concern to downplay circumstantial personal detail in favour of his ideas and art, and I have tried to show above how successful he is in getting his views on politics, crafts and printing across in these interviews. And yet we surely have a good deal of sympathy with Tooley's position here too. Interviews are, in contrast to printed essays, a holistic genre, typically containing their own physical occasion within the text itself; and for us as readers a century or more later it is surely the interplay of context and content, of sensory concretion and intellectual substance, that makes this sequence of interviews with Morris so fascinating.

I stressed above what a symbolic locale Kelmscott House is to many of Morris's visitors, charged with all the complexity and aura of his hybrid identity as Poet–

Socialist. Yet the house and its immediate Hammersmith surroundings are here in memorably humdrum but precise detail too. There is, for example, the old-world iron lantern-holder over the front gate that reminds the *Pall Mall Gazette* reporter of 'the customs of the past', or the notice-board by that very same gate announcing the forthcoming Sunday evening socialist lecture which very decidedly recalls to Sarah Tooley the political urgencies of the present. There is the surprising detail too of the 'semi-grand piano' in the Kelmscott coachhouse or lecture room. Morris isn't by any means alone at Kelmscott House: rather do we get a sense of a busy social and cultural life swirling around him, with Henry Halliday Sparling popping in at one point, various anonymous 'assistants' flitting to and fro, and a curious Jewish delegation who arrive to claim Morris's attention in the *Clarion* interview; the compositors in the nearby Kelmscott Press cottage feature briefly too. The Hammersmith church bell tolls quarter past seven during the *Bookselling* piece, reminding us of the wider neighbourhood beyond the charmed precincts of Morris's study, and several of the reporters respond to the vista of the Thames commanded from Kelmscott House, in moods that range from sensuous delight through patriotic fervour to settled gloom.

Such vivid circumstantial detail attaches not just to the house but to its owner. It is not only Sarah Tooley who describes his clothes – the 'loose navy-blue suit, with a sky-blue shirt well in evidence' – but then this is now a familiar part of our image of Morris. More telling, perhaps, are less predictable details such as the huge walking stick he wields in front of his own tapestry at the 1893 Arts and Crafts exhibition, or the sudden eloquent emission of vast clouds of pipe smoke in the midst of the *Clarion* interview (a quite extraordinary amount of smoking goes on throughout these texts, and not just on Morris's part). We catch some of the distinctive tones and rhythms of Morris's voice here too, in, for example, those 'pithy compact sentences' that so impress the *Daily News* reporter and in the 'terse, rather rugged English' that strikes the 1890 *Cassell's Saturday Journal* interviewer. Such personal idiosyncracies come through also in Morris's fondness for lively 'stories' to drive home a point in these exchanges: the Frenchman who has a lawsuit in Germany, the person who asks what literature is, the Man who Minded the House (who turns up in *News from Nowhere* too). There are certainly times when this energy can become overpowering. When challenged by the *Daily Chronicle* over his backward-looking choice of subjects for tapestry, he launches into what one can only describe as a rant and, as I have suggested above, there is a tendency to browbeat his one female interviewer, to dismiss too brusquely her spirited attempt to champion the woman's cause. Yet there is much of the milk of human kindness coming through in these texts too. I find this most attractively the case in the description of Morris's smiles throughout this sequence, of which there are a good many and of various sorts; the very pulse and flicker of emotion across his features is memorably captured here. So that it is, repeatedly, the circumstantial presence of the man, and not just the force of his thought, which makes these interviews such a vivid introduction to William Morris across the range of his activities in some of the most productive years of his life.

Tony Pinkney

Acknowledgements.
In preparing the notes for this volume I have been greatly indebted to five invaluable tools for Morris research: E.P. Thompson's *William Morris* (1955, revised edition 1976), Norman Kelvin's four volume edition of *The Collected Letters of William Morris* (1984-96), William S. Peterson's *The Kelmscott Press: A History of William Morris's Typographical Adventure* (1991), Fiona MacCarthy's *William Morris: A Life for Our Time* (1994) and Nick Salmon's *The William Morris Chronology* (1996). I have had crucial personal assistance from Peter Faulkner and Bridget Salmon, and I am also grateful to Cornelia Schupp and to my

parents and Justin for their support during my work on this book. I have been selective in my headnotes and footnotes to the interviews, not wanting to overwhelm these relatively short texts with the dead hand of a vast scholarly apparatus. The illustrations are a mix of those that appear in some of the original texts and other relevant images. I am grateful to the British Library, Hammersmith and Fulham Archives, Marx Memorial Library, St Bride Printing Library and the William Morris Gallery for permission to reproduce materials included here. Some aspects of the punctuation of the interviews have been modernised and occasionally corrected, but I have not tried to reduce the disparate house styles of these Victorian newspapers and journals to a single uniform format.

Notes

[1] For a full account of Nick Salmon's Morrisian and other activities, see Peter Faulkner, 'Nicholas Salmon (1957-2001)', *Journal of the William Morris Society*, vol. XIV, no. 4, summer 2002, pp.5-6. A full bibliography of Nick Salmon's Morris publications appears at the end of this volume.

[2] Fiona MacCarthy, *William Morris: A Life for our Time* (London: Faber and Faber, 1994), p.269.

[3] Lucy Brown, *Victorian News and Newspapers* (Oxford: Clarendon Press, 1985), p.160.

[4] See Morris's lecture, 'The Policy of Abstention' (1887), in May Morris, ed., *William Morris: Artist Writer Socialist,* vol. II (Oxford: Basil Blackwell, 1936), pp. 434–53.

[5] William S. Peterson, *The Kelmscott Press: A History of William Morris's Typographical Adventure* (Oxford University Press, 1991), pp.191, 182.

[6] Joseph Dunlap, *The Book That Never Was* (New York: Oriole Editions, 1971).

[7] *Journal of the William Morris Society*, vol. X, no. 4, Spring 1994, p.9.

A Talk with William Morris on Socialism,

Daily News, 8th January 1885, p. 5

The Marxist historian E.P. Thompson once suggested that it was possible to date the effective birth of modern socialism in Britain from 1883. Two years after its emergence it was clearly making enough impact for liberal and radical newspapers to decide to investigate further. The *Daily News* reporter may not be particularly sympathetic to Morris's socialism ('good only for the world of ideas', in his opinion), but he clearly admires Morris himself and gives him the chance to make a wide-ranging statement of his political views, with a particular stress on the 'educational' mission which would come to the fore as Morris left the Social Democratic Federation to found the Socialist League. Morris's first contact with the *Daily News* had been in October 1876 when he published in it his very first letter on public affairs, on 'England and the Turks'. Thereafter he wrote to it regularly, on topics as various as the protection of ancient buildings, the vulgarisation of Oxford, famine in Iceland, the 'malodorous and insanitary condition' of a ditch in Hammersmith, and, of course, socialism.

Just before the prorogation the Earl of Wemyss and

March got up in his place in the House of Lords and flourished a sort of revolutionary symbol in the faces of his meagre but distinguished audience. The symbol, or let me call it paper banner, was *Justice*, not the French journal of the name, but the lively organ of the English Socialists.[1] 'Look at this and tremble,' was the meaning conveyed by his lordship's attitude and brief speech. Some people define English Socialism to be, among other things, 'an attempt to make grand dukes and people of that sort' live on three hundred a year – and work eight hours a day even for that! But on looking at the programme of the Socialists, what I find is a proposal for 'cumulative taxation upon all incomes above a fixed minimum, not exceeding three hundred pounds a year.' However, even the bare suggestion of a squad of dukes working in their shirtsleeves on a tramway (one hour allowed for midday bread and cheese; and half-holiday on Saturday) is so very dreadful (only Mr. Carlyle's notion of a naked House of Lords can match it)[2] that one is not surprised at Lord Wemyss's announcement of his intention to resume the subject when Parliament reassembles. Whether there are English Socialists ready to fulfil their enemies' direst anticipations, or to what extent or in what manner, I do not know. But it occurred to me to 'interview' one who is not only a high priest of Socialism, but also one of the most finely gifted men of his time, and to hear what *he* had to say about it. William Morris, poet, all men know; William Morris, preacher of a new social gospel, poet and prophet (vates) in one, according to antique ideal, fewer know.

I called, found him among his pipes and books, and asked him for some of his own personal impressions and opinions. He promptly plunged *in media res* – giving me to understand beforehand that he was speaking, not in any official capacity, but purely and simply as an individual Socialist. 'I do not care,' he said, 'for a mechanical revolution. I want an educated movement. Discontent is not enough, though it is natural and inevitable. The discontented must know what they are aiming at when they overthrow the old order of things. My belief is that the old order can only be overthrown by force; and for that reason it is all the more necessary that the revolution – for such the movement is, even now – should be, not an ignorant, but an intelligent revolution. What I should like to have now, far more than anything else, would be a body of able, high-minded, competent men, who should act as instructors of the masses and as their leaders during critical periods of the movement. It goes without saying that a great proportion of these instructors and leaders should be working men; even this preliminary movement cannot be carried on far except through them. I should look to these men to preach what Socialism really is – not a change for the sake of change, but a change involving a high and noble, the very noblest, ideal of human life and duty; a life in which every human being should find unrestricted scope for his best powers and faculties. I should like to see two thousand men of that stamp engaged in explaining the principles of rational, scientific Socialism all over the kingdom.'

In advocating his cultured propagandism, Mr. Morris has of course the upper no less than the lower classes in view. Like a brother poet – though perhaps with an intention unlike his – Mr. Morris thinks that the rich classes stand in need of being preached to as well as the poor. He would if he could prepare Mr. Arnold's 'materialised' upper classes for the inevitable day of reckoning.[3] As I have already said, Mr. Morris is not hopeful that the upper classes – the capitalists, agricultural, commercial, and industrial – will be moved by anything short of compulsion; but, on the other hand, much will be gained if the revolution, when it proceeds from speaking to acting, 'can show that it is aiming at a change, the desirability and justice of which can be more or less seen even through the class prejudices of the possessing classes.' 'When,' says Mr. Morris, 'I go about the country I hear people say, "We are miserable; we are about as discontented as we can be; we know the injustice and cruelty of the situation; but tell us what is the best thing

Democratic Federation membership card designed by William Morris. Morris joined the DF in January 1883 and left it in December 1884. (© Marx Memorial Library)

we can do." They cannot know the best thing unless they think clearly and sensitively, and therefore I would help them to acquire right – that is to say, scientific – ideas about the social movement.' One need not talk long with Mr. Morris before one discovers how he resents the impression which prevails in so many quarters that Socialism is an envious, malignant device for crushing out originality, for destroying all the colour and light and joy of existence, and dooming man to bovine toil in a hypochondriacal, drab universe. The bovine toil, which is its own sole end, the joylessness, the drab hue, Mr. Morris would say, exist now; he aspires to relieve them; whatever else he may be, he claims to be a leveller-up.

But not on what Mr. Carlyle calls the principle of 'Devil take the hindmost.' For competition, as practised in modern society, the poet of English Socialism entertains a profound contempt and loathing. Free trade, meaning competition, he regards as the curse of society. In discussing this subject Mr. Morris will rap out some pithy compact sentence, such as the following – 'Competition develops its contradictory,' that is to say, Socialism. 'For what,' he will ask, 'is this competitive Free Trade but a competition, not in the cause of use, but in the cause of profit-mongering? Free Trade is merely free trade in profits; capitalists care for nothing else. The working classes now see this, and have come to understand that their only salvation lies in work, not for the good of this class which cares for nothing but profits; but for the equal good of the whole of society: their ideal is universal use, not class profit, privilege, or monopoly.' I remarked to him that he was just entering upon a subject about which some excellent people, by no means calling themselves Socialists in his sense, would agree with him. 'For example,' I said, 'Mr. Thomas Hughes,[4] who is a Radical, and is, or used to be, a good Free Trader, has just been telling Manchester – of all places in the world! – that competition has only resulted in bringing "the most unscrupulous" to the front; while as for what you say about profit-mongering, how many have complained about the decadence which, in consequence of the China-clay "loading," has come about in our Eastern markets for cotton goods.' 'Oh,' replied Mr. Morris, 'there are many people who will admit the justice of the Socialistic criticisms of the present state of society, and are prepared to do all they can for the working classes that can be done *for* the working classes and not *by* them. In other words, they will favour whatever can be done without altering the present system of capital and wages. In my opinion their hopes are amiable delusions. The maintenance of private property in the means of production – that is land, capital, machinery, & c. – will put a dead stop to any real elevation of the working classes to a higher level. At the same time the opinions of Mr. Thos. Hughes and the co-operators, and indeed of many other social reformers, all tend to show that confidence in the old system is shaken even among the capitalistic classes.' For instance, he remarked that Mr. Ruskin's influence in the propagation of Socialism was far from small.[5] This was in allusion to the great Art Critic's teaching on the use and the nobility of work, and the hatefulness of 'profit-mongering' and usury. He told me that he had found that, in this respect, as well as in others, Mr. Ruskin's influence is especially conspicuous in Edinburgh, where there is a Students' Socialist Society. 'Have Socialistic principles made any headway in the chief towns of Scotland?' I asked. 'Yes', replied Mr. Morris, 'they are making their way in Glasgow, and in Edinburgh there is another besides the Students' Society. Some of the most ardent Socialists are students of the University.' This last statement was new to me, but – I must confess – scarcely surprising; for I remembered how, in other days, I used to hear the most striking doctrines uttered by my theological fellow-men in the corner gallery of the old quadrangle. I was struck, too, by what Mr. Morris said about the tone of Scotch-student Socialism – what there is of it. 'They don't care anything about the merely political questions of Socialism – about legislative machinery and the like; what they do care for is the moral side of it, the introduction of a higher ethics into work and life.' Like, I should imagine, the perfervid race.

'Turning for a moment,' I said, 'to the question of points of contact between your Socialism and political creeds which reject the name, it seems to me that you must find your natural allies in the Radical School of Liberals.'[6] To this Mr. Morris replied: – 'As Radicals they are hard to deal with, many so-called being only an extreme form of Whigs; but of course to many Radicalism is the most progressive thing they have come across as yet, and from these we expect to gain recruits, and do so; only they must give up their Radicalism before they can become Socialists.' From this it is not to be understood that Socialism has made no headway in England; all that Mr. Morris meant was, I think, that English Socialism was of a somewhat sporadic nature, as distinguished from the centralised form of it which exists in Germany – in other words, that English Socialism is not yet properly organized. 'So then,' I said, 'the prospect of the return of Parliamentary candidates on the Socialistic ticket is just now distant.' 'I believe it is,' replied Mr. Morris, 'that is, I cannot conceive of any constituency at the next election returning a Socialist as a Socialist, owing to the above-mentioned want of organization. It is possible that quasi-Socialistic candidates may be put up to make running for the Tory candidate.'[7] And then he rapped out one of those

Socialist League woodcut, designed by Walter Crane, 1885.

pithy sentences to which I have already alluded: 'The Reichstag is the only platform which the German Socialists have from which to assert themselves; in England anybody can say anything anywhere.' And then Mr. Morris entered into an interesting discussion of the reasons why German Socialism has acquired a character so ordered, and rational, and scientific, as compared with some schools of Socialism in other European countries, especially France. 'The nationalising of the army,' said Mr. Morris, 'will produce universal Socialism in Germany, and it will prevent the unarmed and untrained people being kept down by a band of professional soldiers. The repressive laws in Germany have kept the Socialistic party together.'

'Do you think,' I asked, 'that one at least of the motives for the foreign adventures (possibly ending in war) to which foreign states are now committed is the desire to keep down Socialism and other popular movements at home?' 'It may be so,' replied Mr. Morris, 'I have no doubt whatever that all popular movements on the Continent are forms of Socialism. But then the social movement is not merely national; it is international, cosmopolitan, and the instant the masses recognise that wars for "expansion" are anti-international, anti-cosmopolitan - that, in fact, foreign wars are got up by profit-mongers for the good of profit-mongers - the device to which you refer would fail.' Mr. Morris went much further even than that, and he described the Federation cry now heard in England as having been got up in the interests of competition, for the propagation of the doctrine of 'Devil-take-the-hindmost'.

'In Cobden's time,'[8] continued Mr. Morris, 'we did not care for intervention – the Freetraders scouted it, nor did they trouble themselves about Imperial Federation. The reason was that they had command of all the markets of the world; they had no rivals; but now other nations are becoming manufacturing and exporting communities, our markets are becoming smaller and fewer; therefore we now interfere here, there, and everywhere, and we suggest a gigantic union of all the English colonies and dependencies on the mother country. But patriotism has nothing to do with it. The professed patriotism is all a sham – the Federation is solely and simply a refuge for the class of exploiting profit-mongers. You would be surprised to hear,' he said, 'how audiences of working men applaud when I declare these my opinions about the commercial aspects of expansion and our present international politics. The working classes are not Jingoes, whatever persons belonging to other classes may say about them. When the masses in all the European states think consciously together, the end of these market wars will come.' 'What, then,' I said, 'about barbaric races?' 'I would leave them alone,' he replied, 'on this point I agree with the Positivists;[9] I do not see that conquest by civilized nations has done these races any good – it has spoiled them – they have been merely exploited.'

This is only a rough and abbreviated summary of my conversation with Mr. Morris. In the condensed form in which I am obliged to put it it necessarily loses all the fire and eloquence of the speaker's own words. His countrymen may regard his doctrines as impractical and visionary, but there can be no doubt as to the purity and loftiness of the aspiration. 'I hold,' he says, 'that the abolition of classes would tend to the general elevation of all society; would be for the good of the upper as well as the lower; would destroy the precariousness of life now felt by the middle classes as well as others.' Whoever wishes to understand Mr. Morris must bear this in mind: his Socialism is an educational instrument. He would subject every man, woman, and child to the highest, the widest, and the most liberal culture which society could supply, and of which the recipient were capable. Though, as you may think, his views are good only for the world of ideas, there can be no doubt that he is wholly in earnest about them. During the two years which have passed since he declared himself a Socialist, he has been lecturing about the country in public halls, pot-houses, barns, stables, wherever he can find room to stand in, and anybody to listen to him. His lecture-hall at home – 3, Upper Mall, Hammersmith, a quiet, half-rustic spot, within a few yards of the placid, turbid Thames – is an old stable, which he has comfortably fitted up and transformed for its novel purpose. There is more room there for an audience than elsewhere on the premises. Having undertaken his social task, he enters into it with all his might. Not only is he an indefatigable lecturer, he is an omnivorous student of his subject. He has the literature of Socialism at his finger-ends. He is the Socialist even in such pure formalities as the disuse of merely conventional titles. For instance, if you or I should ever become a member of some Socialistic society we should drop the 'esquire' in writing to him through the penny or half-penny post, and address him simply as William Morris. In the Socialistic system there is no room for esquires, or barons, or grand dukes, but only for 'citizens,' 'brothers,' 'comrades.'

Referring to a report that a schism had taken place in the Social Democratic Federation, I asked Mr. Morris if it was correct. 'Yes,' he replied; 'there has been a split, I am sorry to say. Some of us felt that there was an attempt to rule the Social Democratic Federation arbitrarily, and to drag it towards political opportunism tinctured with Jingoism.[10] The rent in the body produced by this could not be plastered over, and very unwillingly I am compelled to take sides, and am one of the seceders. We have formed a new body called the Socialist League, and shall have a paper of our own. We uphold the purest doctrines of scientific Socialism, and shall educate and organize towards the fundamental change in society of which I have spoken. Once more, let me impress this upon you: The working classes must understand that they are not appendages of capital. When the change comes it will embrace the whole of society, and there will be no discontented class left to form the elements of a fresh revolution. This is what I meant when I began by saying that I did not want a mechanical revolution – such as would happen if only a small minority were to overthrow the established government, and to attempt to rule by the permanent exercise of mere brute force.'

Notes

[1] *Justice* was the weekly newspaper of the Social Democratic Federation; its first issue appeared on 19th January 1884. H. M. Hyndman's autocratic editing of it was one of the bones of contention that led Morris and others to break with the SDF.

[2] Thomas Carlyle (1795–1881), historian and social critic, the archetypal 'Victorian sage'. His *Past and Present* (1843), contrasting Victorian capitalism unfavourably with medieval life and society, influenced Morris and Burne-Jones at Oxford.

[3] Matthew Arnold (1822–88), poet, literary and social critic, and inspector of schools. Much of his work seeks to inject 'sweetness and light' into what he saw as the narrowed, philistine perspectives of the English middle class.

[4] Thomas Hughes (1822–96), Christian Socialist and later Liberal M.P., author of *Tom Brown's Schooldays* (1856).

[5] John Ruskin (1819–1900), critic of art, architecture and society. His *The Seven Lamps of Architecture* (1849), *Modern Painters* (1843–60) and *The Stones of Venice* (1851–3) influenced Morris deeply at Oxford.

[6] The Liberal Party was formed in the mid-Victorian period as an amalgam of Whigs (its landed, upper-class element), new industrialists, professional men, and Radicals.

[7] I.e., by dividing the Liberal vote. This did in fact happen, in the so-called 'Tory Gold' episode in the 1885 general election, where two Social Democratic Federation candidates were funded by the Tories.

[8] Richard Cobden (1804–65), established the Anti-Corn Law League in 1839, M.P. for Stockport from 1841, advocate of free trade.

[9] The leader of the English Positivists was Frederic Harrison (1831–1923). He regarded positivism not just as a philosophical position (denying validity to all knowledge not derived from the senses) but also as a commitment to social reform. He therefore pressed for wider primary education, extension of the franchise and enlightened labour legislation.

[10] The following day the *Daily News* contained a letter by H. H. Champion of the Social Democratic Federation rebutting Morris's charges. The *Saturday Review* printed a hostile anonymous review of the interview on 10th January. Its author maintains that 'Mr. Morris cannot look out of his window, or into his looking-glass, or back over his life without seeing how flatly contrary to the whole course of nature and experience … is this cloud castle of his'.

The Poet and the Police:
An Interview with
Mr. William Morris,

Pall Mall Gazette, 23rd September 1885, p. 4.

On 20th September 1885 a large crowd assembled at the intersection of Dod Street and Burdett Road in Limehouse, in London's East End, to be addressed by Radical, Social Democratic Federation and Socialist League speakers. As the meeting was dispersing the police attacked it and arrested eight people. The scenes in the Thames Police Court the following day, under the magistrate Thomas William Saunders, are vividly recounted by Morris in the course of this interview, which also contains his more general reflections on the campaign for free speech in the mid-1880s. The magistrate's lenient treatment of Morris, in stark contrast to his tough sentences on the working-class comrades, led to the *Funny Folks* 'Attitude of the Police' cartoon which we reprint below. The *Pall Mall Gazette* under the editorship of W.T. Stead, though a liberal rather than a socialist newspaper, was strongly critical of the police persecution of open-air political meetings. H.M.Hyndman, leader of the Social Democratic Federation, had himself once worked on the *Pall Mall Gazette* and noted in his *Record of an Adventurous Life*

(1911) that 'it allowed free expression to out-and-out democratic opinion ably expressed'.

A representative of the *Pall Mall Gazette* called yesterday afternoon upon Mr. William Morris at his fine-art works at Merton Abbey, and at his invitation Mr. Morris willingly 'thought aloud' at greater length than the officers of Mr. Saunders's court would permit, upon the subject of the police and their prosecutions.

'The *Standard*, I see,' he observed, 'speaks of the magistrate's decision being "in accordance with justice and common sense;"[1] but I will be bound that if the writer had been present in court yesterday he would not have thought so. The fact is, the worthy magistrate picked out for discharge the man who did the most, while he sent to prison for two months the man who was least responsible. We are really concerned for Lyons, who is not the sort of fellow to have done the thing charged against him.[2] The constable charged Lyons with having kicked him, but how could the policeman tell absolutely who kicked him in a crowd like that? The evidence given in support of the attempt to connect the banner-bearers with a previous resistance to the police was most trumpery, and if I had been a juryman I should not have convicted upon it, even supposing that the police were in a position to identify those men in the midst of a great crowd when they were almost the breadth of a street away. From what I know of the people taken, I feel certain that they had not been active in the matter. We are bound, I think, to take what action may be possible to secure the release of Lyons.

'When I found myself in the dock, my word it was so absurd a charge that I really did not know what to say. I could not treat it seriously. When the sentence was passed upon the men charged with resisting the police we had all cried out "Shame!" and then came the order, "Clear the court!" Two or three policemen rushed at us, especially the policeman who had given evidence against Lyons. He caught hold of me and shoved me, and also seized Mrs.

Aveling by the shoulder, and hustled us about.[3] I had previously said, "All right, I am going," and all that I did when hustled, was what a man always does when shoved - he stiffens himself up, else he would fall down. Turning round, I remonstrated with the constable upon his conduct, when he exclaimed "I will run you in," and then, as if a brilliant idea had suddenly struck him, he added, "you have broken my helmet chin-strap." Thereupon, another bobby having taken hold of me, they ran me into the road, where the people cheered me vigorously. I was walked into the police-station, where there was some ridiculous discussion as to the damage to the helmet; and afterwards I was kept for two hours in the lobby before I was placed in the dock. I am sorry for more reasons than one that I answered the magistrate's inquiry – "What are you?" - in the language I did.[4] As a sure as a gun, if I had passed as an ordinary workman, I would have been sent to

Sketch by Walter Crane of William Morris addressing a May Day rally. (© William Morris Gallery)

prison. Yes, your contemporary's "empty-headed artists and literary men" is one for me; but I am tolerably thick-skinned. By the way, I was congratulated at our meeting last night on having written a new poem.'

'I shall probably go to prison yet,' continued Mr. Morris, 'if the authorities maintain their present attitude. I have to go to Manchester next Sunday, but the Sunday after, if the game is kept up, I am bound to be on the ground. But I honestly confess I do not take kindly to the idea of going to gaol. Besides, I have read the article in the *Pall Mall Gazette* by a writer who had spent some days in Holloway Gaol. The fines of all the men who were fined were paid the same evening, but not so quickly as to prevent one of them having his hair cropped; and after they had been committed, they were insulted most grossly by the police. Going to gaol, even for a week, is no joke for these working men, as we must all admit if we give the matter a thought; but they are very eager in this business, I assure you. The existence of this spirit of self-sacrifice on the part of the working men makes the position of some difficulty for persons with means. I have not yet made up my mind what course I should take if I were simply fined. My view is that everybody ought to do in this matter as his conscience bids him. We are certainly determined to support our friends. It grieves me to see so many outsiders taken, for all the speakers were not taken. We ought all to be taken.'

Invited to express his views upon the conflict in its graver aspects, Mr. Morris said, 'We are regarding it simply from the public-meeting point of view. The movement at present represented in Burdett-road is not necessarily a Socialist movement; it is a movement in defence of the right of free speech. As I have heard the law expounded, those who call a meeting on a public road hold it on peril of being charged with causing an obstruction - with preventing a person going anywhere he pleases on the road; but before a conviction is entered, there certainly ought to be good proof of actual obstruction - the obstruction ought not to be a merely technical obstruction, but a real obstruction. Whether meetings held in the street shall be interfered with or not undoubtedly lies largely in the discretion of the authorities for each district. But it is not the custom to strain the laws against the promoters of these meetings unless the necessities of the public convenience imperatively call for interference. At Hammersmith, where we have held the meetings on a piece of waste ground beside the road, the police were even good enough to say, at a time when we were troubled with ill-mannered opposition, that if we sent them word they would send round constables to maintain order for us. The police of the East-end, however, appear to be downright ill-tempered. I suppose the police grow worse when they have continually to deal with poor people, for down there they seem to treat the people like dogs. The Socialist League has been "warned" in Soho and Hoxton, and interfered with at Stratford, and, in this present case, at Limehouse. But when we were interfered with at Stratford, Mr. Phillips decided that there had been no obstruction proved, and discharged the prisoner. As everybody knows, meetings of other kinds have been held in numberless places without interference for years and years. We contend that the persistent interference with the Socialist meetings held in Dod-street proves an animus of some sort, wherever it comes from - which we don't profess to know. A police-officer with whom I talked on the subject at the police-court raised what might be regarded as a reasonable objection - that meetings in the street interfered with the rest of working people who had to sleep during the day; but when I asked him, "Then why have you not shut up the 'Salvationists'?" he immediately shifted his ground, saying, "You must admit that the people of this country as a body are religious." That observation, as I remarked to the officer, just proves our case. We are interfered with because we preach disagreeable doctrines.

'The good magistrate asks, "If you want to preach your doctrines, why don't you hire halls or go to the parks?" Well, the working people who form the Socialist bodies do not hire halls because they cannot afford to do so, and they do not confine themselves to the parks because they cannot there reach all the classes of people whom they wish to reach. The people who most need to be stirred to a comprehension of their own condition are the very people who do not and will not attend ordinary meetings, whether in hall or park. We must get at these people at their own doors, and these are the people we do get at by our street meetings. They are so down-drawn with poverty that they scarcely know what to think at first, but they always listen patiently and quietly. When there are

disturbances they are caused by men in better positions. If we do not get hold of these poor people, what can we do? They are the people who have the best reason to be discontented – they are the people who must move. Other missionary organizations will appreciate this as readily as the Socialists. Apart altogether from the objects of the promoters, I believe that the stoppage of these meetings would entail upon the people a distinct loss. I think in respect to these meetings in the same way as I think in regard to the complaints against the street musicians – how wearisome and dull the streets would be if they were as respectable people would have them! For myself, I would rather experience some noise and suffering rather than that the streets should be dull. We must remember that the people in the poorer districts have not the same recreations and amusements that we possess.

'The movement as a movement for the defence of free speech is now in the hands of a vigilance committee, formed of delegates from political clubs and leagues; and I should think the suggestion made by the *Pall Mall Gazette* – for the summoning of a conference of all persons interested in the maintenance of the right to hold public meetings in the streets – will commend itself to the committee. Unless the Home Secretary intervenes, I have no doubt that we shall be interfered with next Sunday.[5]

Police attacking marchers on 'Bloody Sunday', 13th November 1887.
Engraving in *The Graphic*, 19th November 1887.
(© British Library)

The men who attend these meetings may be as peaceably disposed as you please, but when a man is knocked down, who can answer for him? However, if the peace is broken, the burden will lie solely upon the police. It may be that the Government, having been rather loose in one direction – Ireland – are pulling the reins a little tighter in another direction, in order to regain their character for firmness. Still, it cannot be in the interests of the Government to allow this business to continue. As one of my workmen remarked to me this morning, every Conservative candidate at the East End will rapidly lose any chances of election they may have had.' 'As I have said,' concluded Mr. Morris, 'I am not predisposed to enjoy the luxury of martyrdom in a small way, but I am quite clear that the question must be fought out, whatever may be the cost.' 'Have you any important literary work in hand at present, Mr. Morris?' 'I cannot say that I have – I cannot find time.' 'Then it may be a public gain if you are put into prison?' 'Ah! But there is the oakum to pick.'[6]

Notes

[1] In its issue for Tuesday 22nd September the *Standard* announced that 'the time for toleration is past': 'the claim of a Socialist, or any other man, to obstruct the streets whenever and wherever he wants to deliver a speech is one that cannot be allowed, and the decisions of the magistrate yesterday were in strict accordance with both justice and common sense'.

[2] Lewis Lyons, an East End tailor, was sentenced to two months hard labour by Saunders for kicking a policeman. The sentence was quashed on appeal.

[3] Eleanor Marx Aveling (1855-98), daughter of Karl Marx and a leading member of the Socialist League.

[4] Morris had replied: 'I am an artist, and a literary man, pretty well known, I think, throughout Europe'.

[5] In fact, an enormous crowd – of between thirty and forty thousand people – turned up at Dod Street the next Sunday. Radical and socialist speakers addressed them and the police prudently remained on the sidelines. However, police attacks on socialist meetings did resume thereafter, particularly after the 'Black Monday' riot of 8th February 1886, and in July 1886 Morris was summoned for obstructing the highway at Bell Street on the 18th. At his trial six days later he was fined one shilling.

[6] Oakum is the loose fibre got by picking old rope to pieces. The task was assigned to convicts and paupers.

Representative Men at Home: Mr. William Morris at Hammersmith,

Cassell's Saturday Journal,
18th October 1890, pp. 80-2.

Cassell's Saturday Journal was a genial Victorian miscellany, containing serialised stories and an extraordinary variety of lightweight journalism. Among the other contents of its October 18th 1890 issue are 'Animals and their Dislikes', 'Some Strange Adventures in Soho' and 'Funeral Customs of the Poor'. Its 'Representative Men at Home' series was at the weightier end of the spectrum of its offerings, though even here the 'at home' emphasis domesticates the moral, literary and political issues the interviews raise. Other Victorian luminaries who featured in the series included John Ruskin, Samuel Smiles, Henry Arthur Jones and Sir Edward Arnold. The interview with Morris, which includes a fulsome tribute to Karl Marx, has been an important reference point in subsequent debates as to whether Morris's variety of socialism was or was not Marxist.

Mr. William Morris's house bears the mark of its occupant both outside and in. On the gates of a side building that once formed a stable and coachhouse, one reads notices of Democratic Federation meetings held within, and one raps at the door by a knocker highly suggestive of art workmanship, and the original of which may have come from the hands of some mediæval chaser. The hall inside is adorned with wood engravings from the drawings of Albert Durer;[1] and the furniture of the house, so far as the casual visitor has opportunity of observing, is quite unique.

These are matters which one cannot but feel some difficulty and delicacy in discussing. There are some sturdy souls who do not mind going into a man's house and bringing away with them a full and complete catalogue of his furniture for the interest of a curious, and perhaps hypercritical, world. Not unto all of us is it given to do this without misgiving, and in a general way it is perhaps best to be content with discussing the man himself. But in the case of one like Mr. Morris, whose name is so intimately associated with the arts of domestic decoration, it may be permissible to allude for a moment to the strikingly original style of furniture.

The drawing room, Kelmscott House, Hammersmith, London (© St Bride Printing Library).

Take, for instance, his dining room, an apartment on the ground floor at the back of the house. On being introduced into this room, a corner of which is shown by our artist in his smaller drawing, one's first momentary impression is that he is entering the kitchen. This impression is derived mainly from two objects, which are sufficiently conspicuous to give character to the room. One is a drab-coloured 'dresser,' with an array of willow-pattern plate upon its shelves – that is how it strikes the visitor who sees it for the first time; and the other is a heavy, uncovered, deal-topped table that has been scrubbed white – that is what one takes it for. The visitor, moreover, is asked to take his seat in a slight black-framed armchair with an old-fashioned rush bottom.

A glance round, however, is sufficient to show that it is not a rather plainly furnished kitchen, but a sumptuously furnished dining room. On a closer scrutiny the 'dresser' becomes a severely artistic sideboard, and the willow-patterned plates are found to be old blue ware, every piece of which has its own pattern and its individual merits. A miscellaneous collection of jugs and jars is perceived to be a number of vases of rare design and varied material. The top shelf is surmounted by two or three exquisite specimens of bronze work, and the dull blue of the plate spread out on the lower shelves is relieved by a touch of intense colour in two large vases of majolica ware by the ends of the sideboard. Similarly the deal-topped table resolves itself into a massive piece of workmanship, all in solid oak, the underpart being varnished, but the top merely bound round with a band of iron at its edge, and left to be scoured with the scrubbing brush.

Besides these articles of furniture, there is on one side of the room a handsome-looking coffer, adorned with some very choice specimens of metal work, and above this is suspended a fine Persian carpet, perhaps a couple of hundred years old. The upper portion of the walls is papered with a dull bluish green; the lower part is wainscoted in drab. The large window is rather baldly draped in curtains in a dull blue and red. The floor is polished, and here and there covered with an oriental rug;

there is a couch of classic simplicity of form, covered with material, the colour of which is apparently to correspond with that of the old blue china on the sideboard; there is a deep easy armchair similarly covered; there are two or three solid-looking old oak chairs, and others for ordinary use of the rush-bottomed type already alluded to. This remarkable room is further embellished by several family portraits by Rossetti – all of them very masterly pieces of work, but all of them characterised by that inscrutable, melancholy sort of mysticism with which Rossetti's eye seemed always to invest even the brightest and fairest of faces.[2]

It is a striking and interesting room, but there is an air of Spartan severity and simplicity about it – a certain austerity amounting almost to gloom. Frankly speaking, it is not what everybody would care to call his dining room; one wants to be educated up to it, and it is only right to say that Mr. Morris himself seems hardly to be satisfied with it, and gives his visitor to understand that when he came into the house he found this a sombre and ill-proportioned apartment, and had to make the best of it. One is rather relieved to hear this, because it seems to justify the opinion one has formed upon the subject; and Mr. Morris has won so great a name and fame for his taste in domestic decoration that one naturally distrusts his own judgement if he cannot fully and cordially appreciate any work in which so great an authority has been so much interested as he would naturally be in his own home. Moreover, Mr. Morris is a man with whom one instinctively feels some diffidence in opposing any matter of taste or opinion. Personally he gives you the impression of a strong, resolute, eminently capable man. His strongly marked face, his high, broad forehead, surmounted by a rather shaggy, dishevelled head of hair, and the vigorous restlessness with which he twists about in his chair as he talks to you, or walks rapidly up and down the room – all convey the impression of a man of superabounding energy, both of mind and body, no less than the terse, rather rugged English in which on occasion he can give expression to his opinion.

It is an old-fashioned house in which the author of 'The Defence of Guenevere,' 'The Earthly Paradise,' and 'Chants for Socialists' has lived for the past eleven years. In front it overlooks the river just above Hammersmith Bridge, and at the back it has one of those great green gardens which are now, alas!, to be found only here and there about surburban London.

'I have come to see you, Mr. Morris,' begins his visitor, 'not so much as an artist and a poet, and as the head of a famous business; but more particularly as the high priest of Socialism.'

'Take a cigarette and come into the garden,' is the rejoinder. 'We can walk about there and talk.'

We stroll out accordingly over a sheet of such turf as one rarely meets with except in such places as some of the old college gardens in Oxford, or the old secluded enclosures lying under the shadows of Canterbury Cathedral; and for a while we go wandering round, talking about the fine trees that are rustling in the sunshine, and the beds of lilies and roses that seem to have things all their own way in this verdant wilderness which the artist owner possibly enjoys all the more from his having little time to attend to it.

Kelmscott House, Upper Mall, Hammersmith. Morris's home from 1878 till his death in 1896.
(© Hammersmith & Fulham Archives).

'How long have you been a Socialist, Mr. Morris?'

'Well, really, I can hardly say.'

'From time immemorial, eh?'

'No, not exactly that. I began to take an active interest in Socialism – let me see – I think it must have been in 1882. But I had been a Socialist a long time before that.'

'What was it inclined you that way?'

'Oh, I had for a long time given a good deal of attention to social problems, and I got hold of a copy of Carl Marx's work in French; unfortunately I don't read German. It was Carl Marx, you know, who originated the present Socialist movement; at least, it is pretty certain that that movement would not have gathered the force it has done if there had been no Carl Marx to start it on scientific lines.'

'Be good enough, Mr. Morris, to give the readers of the SATURDAY JOURNAL Carl Marx's teaching in a nutshell.'

'The general purpose of his great work is to show that Socialism is the natural outcome of the past. From the entire history of the past, he shows that it is a mere matter of evolution, and that, whether you like it or whether you don't, you will have to have it; that just as chattel slavery gave way to mediæval feudalism, and feudalism to free competition, so the age of competition must inevitably give way to organism. It is the natural order of development.'

'The present competitive system of society is a necessary and inevitable stage in a process of evolution?'

'Just so.'

'Well, seeing that this is the case, don't you think that the fact that the present system of things *is* necessary and inevitable ought to moderate the ferocity of some of your Socialist fire eaters? Why should capitalists be denounced as thieves, and private enterprise as a system of swindling, if it is all part and parcel of a social order in process of evolution?'

'Well, it must very much depend upon whether or not they know what they are doing. Many people are appropriating what really belongs to others without being aware of it. No doubt it is wrong to impute moral blame to them. But there are many who are perfectly well aware of the injustice of the system of which they form a part, but who hold on to it, and do their best to perpetuate and maintain it, from purely selfish motives. They are grasping that which really belongs to another, and they know it. Morally they are thieves in the strictest and most literal sense of the word.'

'But, Mr. Morris, I know those who say that you yourself are tarred with the same brush. As the head of a manufacturing concern you are an employer of operatives, a capitalist, working on the competitive system. What, they ask, is the difference between you and the wicked world?'

'The difference is this: that while I believe the competitive system to be wrong, I am doing my best to sweep it away and set up what I believe to be right in the place of it; my individualist critics are equally well aware that the present system is wrong, but they are doing their best to defend and perpetuate it.'

'Meanwhile, they say, you ought to publicly share whatever you have got, and run your concern for the good of the community.'

'What good should I do by that? I am not fighting individuals, I am attacking a system. How could I attack it more effectually by reducing myself to the proletariat level?'

'Have you any sort of official connection with Socialism, Mr. Morris?'

'I am a member of the Socialist League, that is all. Till recently I edited the *Commonweal*; but I have given that up.[3] I write for it, but I don't edit it.'

'How is that? The Socialists are reputed to be rather a quarrelsome fraternity. People say you are always splitting.'

'Why, of course we are. That is because we have strong convictions. We split because we are earnest and really alive. If we were apathetic and indifferent we shouldn't split. There are two main sources of dispute. We cannot quite agree as to what is likely to be the best social system of the future, and we cannot agree as to the best method of attaining it. But these are matters that will work themselves out as we go along.'

'You really are going along? You have no doubt Socialism is making real progress?'

'Not the least. The working classes are being thoroughly permeated by Socialist ideas. It is that which has given such a totally new significance to all the recent strikes.[4] Till lately a successful strike for higher wages was an end in itself. Men got the advance they asked for and that was that. The significance of the recent strikes is that they have all been part of a great movement. They have been means to a further advance. Everybody has felt that there was something to follow.'

'Yes, it is that vague apprehension of what is to follow that has so frightened people.'

'There is nothing to be frightened at. Nobody will be hurt unless they are fools enough to set themselves against irresistible forces, and then, of course, they must expect to be.'

'You don't, then, apprehend any revolutionary upstir?'

'I think it is very likely that there will by-and-by be a bit of a flare-up when public opinion is quite ripe for a change. But it will be nothing very alarming. In the ordinary course of things profits are everywhere being gradually reduced; competition is becoming keener, and the struggle for a living among capitalists harder. The capitalist's position, in short, will become less and less worth fighting for. Then probably will come some sort of test struggle. There will be a feeling that capital must make its final stand: and if it loses, then it will be perceived that it is really of no use fighting further. The whole thing will collapse, and changes will come very swiftly.'

'And have you made your house here a centre of the Socialist propaganda?'

'Yes, this is my conventicle where we hold public meetings every Sunday evening, and meetings of the League privately once a week.'

And Mr. Morris leads the way in from the garden by a little whitewashed door into the little lecture hall or 'conventicle' shown in one of our engravings. As has already been said, it has been formed out of a stable and coachhouse. Its whitewashed walls have been covered round with a dado of matting; it has a supply of Windsor chairs; there is a semi-grand piano, on which lie furled one or two red flags, and there is a small collection of miscellaneous books – a few novels and biographies, histories and general scientific treatises, and it need hardly be said a good many works on social science – Mill's 'Political Economy,' Seaman's 'Progress of Nations,' the two recent Reports on the Sweating System, the system of land tenure in various countries and so forth.[5]

'And have you a large circle of Socialists round here, Mr. Morris?'

'Our branch of the Socialist League has absorbed the greater part of those in the neighbourhood, and especially members of the Radical Club, who were once active Radicals.'

And with that comes to an end an 'interview' to which, it must be said, Mr. Morris has consented with some reluctance, and for the report of which it is only fair to state that he is not responsible.

Notes

[1] Albrecht Dürer (1471-1528), German painter and engraver. Morris and Burne-Jones were fascinated by his work from their Oxford student days onwards.

[2] Dante Gabriel Rossetti (1828-82), poet and painter, one of the founding members of the Pre-Raphaelite Brotherhood. Rossetti exercised a charismatic influence over the young Morris and Burne-Jones in the late 1850s, and later became the lover of Morris's wife, Jane.

[3] Morris was ejected from the editorship of *Commonweal* in May 1890 as the Socialist League came more and more under anarchist control.

[4] In the late 1880s unskilled workers were organising themselves into trade unions for the first time. Of the great Dock Strike of 1889 Morris wrote in *Commonweal*: 'it is just this element of conscious or semi-conscious attack on the slave-drivers generally which distinguishes this strike from the usual trade union bickerings'.

[5] John Stuart Mill, *Principles of Political Economy* (1848); Ezra C. Seaman, *Essays on the Progress of Nations* (1846).

The Poet as Printer: An Interview with Mr. William Morris,

Pall Mall Gazette, 12th November 1891, pp. 1-2.

The *Pall Mall Gazette*'s interest in Morris was never just political. Already in 1886 its editor, W.T. Stead, had invited him, along with Ruskin, Swinburne and others, to recommend his one hundred favourite books to its readership. Press interest in Morris's plans for printing was intense, from the first mention of his proposed reprint of *The Golden Legend* in the 'Literary Gossip' section of the *Athenaeum* in September 1890 onwards. Indeed, it was the frenzied response to the *Athenaeum*'s subsequent announcement early in 1891 of the imminent appearance of *The Story of the Glittering Plain* from the Kelmscott Press that persuaded Morris to print two hundred copies of the book, rather than just the twenty copies for friends he had originally planned. Though the *Pall Mall Gazette* reporter here does not have the specialist bibliophilic knowledge of Morris's later interviewer from *Bookselling*, he does none the less prompt his subject into giving a genial introductory exposition of the principles of the Kelmscott Press.

'The houses on the opposite bank are very ugly. They remind me of children crying over an arithmetic lesson.

Otherwise the view is not bad from here, and if you turn to the right you look into the foliage of the big trees in Battersea Park,' said Mr. William Morris as we stood in front of Kelmscott House, Hammersmith, and watched the grey light on the river. Everybody at Hammersmith knows Kelmscott House and Mr. Morris (writes a representative). A one-eyed grimy bargeman, whom I encountered in one of the labyrinthine passages of the neighbourhood, hailed with delight the opportunity of directing anybody to the centre of Socialism. 'Mr. Morris's house? Why, bless you, of course I know it. Come down into the yard by the river, and I'll show you exactly where it is. You couldn't miss it.'

There is nothing remarkable about the outside of Kelmscott House. It is square and high, like some of its neighbours, and over the front gate an old-world iron lantern-holder tells of the customs of the past. But as soon as you open the front door you are in another world. Rows of pictures meet the eye as you enter, and you have a vision of old oak, wrought iron, and shelves and shelves of bulky old volumes, arranged not as if they were part and parcel of a 'show-library,' but as if they were in daily, hourly use. Such is indeed the case, and it is they, or some of them, which formed the model for Mr. Morris's beautiful new volume of his 'Poems by the Way,' of which a review appeared in our columns a few days ago.[1]

'I cannot see how we could do better than go back to the Roman type of the fourteenth century,' said Mr. Morris, restlessly walking up and down in his work-room, where more old oak, more quaint china and pottery, more beautiful pictures attract at every turn. The art treasures are arranged with a quasi-carelessness which is more effective than the most elaborate setting and gives a peculiar charm to the large, lofty room. 'The typographic art is, of course, limited. You have the alphabet to work on. The chief object is to make the type as legible as possible, and as beautiful. Now, it seems to me that the Venetians of the fifteenth century attained the highest perfection in typographic art, and after careful comparisons I selected the type of a Venetian volume of the fifteenth century as a model for my book. Let me show it to you.'

And from his treasury in the hall Mr. Morris brought one old brown tome after the other, each beautifully preserved; each showing in progressive line a step from the old, uneven Gothic characters towards the clear Roman characters, and each in itself a treasure. The last in the line was 'Opus Nicolai Jansonis Gallici.'[2]

'This I consider the most perfect specimen of Roman typography,' Mr. Morris went on. 'I have taken it as the model for my book, although I have not followed it servilely. Where I thought I could improve, I have done so; but those old Venetians who perfected the Roman type knew very well what they were about, and there was no need for altering much. Look at the paper too. It is beautiful. Of course, handmade. The paper, too, has been my model. Now just compare the two, and you will see.' The dainty, light volume of 'Poems by the Way' looked like a snowdrop by the side of a gigantic sunflower as it lay on the table next to old Janson's massive book, but all the same the similarity between the two books was striking. The same clear, even type, the same mellow tone of the paper, the same deep black ink, and the same innumerable marks of watchful care over all the details by which a book is made beautiful. 'England has always been the worst of all languages for typography. It was the Italians and the Germans who were most perfect in the art up to about the fifteenth century. Then they too began to go down, and in the seventeenth century only France and Holland had anything to boast of in the way of printing. Look at the books we turn out in this country nowadays. No book ought to be printed with smaller type than that which I am now using. Even the books of our best authors are spoiled by the type. Look at Mr. Ruskin's works. They are about the worst printed and ugliest looking books in the language.'

'But you are about to remedy the defect – at least, partly – are you not, Mr. Morris, by printing part of the "Stones of Venice"?'

'Yes, just one chapter of it. The one "On the Nature of Gothic," which is really the kernel of the whole work.[3] In it Ruskin summarises all he has to say on architecture. If larger and better type were generally adopted, there would be an initial expense for the type, and that would be comparatively large; but think of the benefit that would be conferred on the public! No more of the horrible type and cheap editions which the millions now have to read, and by which they spoil their eyesight.'

'But, Mr. Morris, is it not better to give them books with small type, which they can buy cheap, than to prevent them from reading at all, which would be the case if there were no small type and consequent cheap editions?'

'Well, yes, that is where the difficulty lies. You see,' Mr. Morris went on, with a sudden smile flitting over his face as he turned to the old, old story, 'you see if we were all Socialists things would be different. We should have a public library at each street corner, where everybody should read all the best books, printed in the best and most beautiful type. I should not then have to buy all these old books, but they would be common property, and I could go and look at them whenever I wanted them, as would everybody else. Now I have to go to the British Museum, which is an excellent institution, but it is not enough. I want these books close at hand, and frequently, and therefore I must buy them. It is the same with everybody else, and if they have not money enough to buy them they must go without. Socialism would alter all that.'

'It would give us a hundred British Museums instead of the one, you mean, Mr. Morris?'

'Just so. But come and let me show you my printing press. It is close by, a small place, and I shall try to keep it as small as possible. A large business takes too much time.' A small place, indeed, it is. There, near the window in the lower room, stands the hand press, an almost exact model of the olden days of Caxton, Gutenberg, Schoeffer, Coster and Castaldi.[4] A volume of Mr. Wilfred Blunt's poems is in hand;[5] sheet after sheet is 'pulled' with square blank spaces for the red initials. Upstairs the compositors, a woman compositor among their number, are at work with 'The Golden Legend,' pages of which, hanging like wet linen on clothes lines, fill another room. And all in the clear, bold type of 'Poems by the Way.'

'What about the purely ornamental part of your books, Mr. Morris? About the ornamental borders and initials; are the designs also rescued from the abyss of time, or are they your own designs?'

'All the designs are my own, but I have been guided in my designs by those in the old books. Yes, you can take one to reproduce in the *Pall Mall Budget*. Take this T, we can't spare an S, ever so many characters in "The Golden Legend," which I am printing for Mr. Quaritch,[6] begin with an S. It is all "Saint" this and that and the other. The other letter most frequently required is A, "And it is to wyte:" "And we ought to note," "And the cause wherefore," and so on, from first to last.'

'Then, in your opinion, the ornamental initials of the fifteenth century are superior to those designed by the artists of the present day?'

Mr. Morris shook his head, and smiled his quiet smile. 'Every cock crows on his own tub. I may think so, but it is not for me to pronounce an opinion. The public must judge for themselves in this matter.'

'And now, Mr. Morris, tell me of your Chaucer.[7] What is the edition you intend publishing to be like? Old English or modern, bowdlerized or uncorrupted, including the things of which the authorship is questionable, or strictly adhering to what is Chaucer's beyond a doubt?'

'Old English, of course, and certainly not bowdlerized. I think I shall include the "Romaunt of the Rose," and in fact everything that is generally included in a good edition of Chaucer. It is very difficult to get a thoroughly good edition, and to know exactly what to include. Good work in clearing up the mystery has been done in our days. Look at Dr. Furnivall and others.[8] Still, it is not easy. I have a good seventeenth century edition; wait, and I'll show it you.'

It was a beauty, date 1602: a volume to covet. And from it we dipped into other ancient tomes, many of them with the mark of the chain by which they had been fastened in their youthful days still upon them. But in their old age they live a life of perfect liberty, standing carelessly in long rows, or laying about in a black oak press that dates perchance from the same period as some of them.

'Here is a curious old German work,' Mr. Morris went on, with the evident delight of a true lover of old books, to whom his treasures are a never-ceasing source of enjoyment. 'Some old chap has made marginal remarks in it which are sometimes very curious. Look here, for instance; this passage refers to some German prince, and the old fellow has written *falsum est* after it.'

Mr. Morris read the passage of Early German with as much ease as he reads quaint mediæval Latin and Italian. 'But I can't manage modern German,' he said, as we turned over the leaves and lingered over the grotesque, suggestive old cuts. 'It beats me altogether. In early German there is no syntax. I see no other reason for going to war with Germany than their horrible syntax. It is true, they might retaliate, and say that, where they sin in syntax, we do the same in our spelling. You know the story of the Frenchman who had a lawsuit in Germany, don't you? The lawyer for the other side was pleading, and the Frenchman kept on asking his lawyer, "What does he say? What does he say?" but the lawyer only answered, "Hush, hush, I can't tell you just yet. I am waiting for the verb." That is what it is. It is the scattered verbs that beat us.'

Notes

1 Morris's *Poems by the Way*, a collection of his later verse, was the second book from the Kelmscott Press, appearing in October 1891. The *Pall Mall Gazette* reviewed it on November 2nd. Generally positive, the review does none the less contain a significant caveat: 'we are a little inclined, now and then, to rebel against the large initials, graceful though they be in design. Extending halfway across the page, they disturb the lineation of the verse, and render it impossible for the eye to take in at a glance the metrical scheme, the contour of the stanza'.

2 The work of the fifteenth-century Venetian printer, Nicolas Jenson, served Morris as a model for his Roman or 'Golden' type (so named because he intended to print Jacobus de Voragine's *The Golden Legend* in it).

3 *The Nature of Gothic: A Chapter of the Stones of Venice* was issued from the Kelmscott Press in March 1892. In his preface Morris memorably termed it 'one of the very few necessary and inevitable utterances of the century'.

4 From May 1891 the Kelmscott Press occupied Sussex Cottage, 14 Upper Mall, Hammersmith, just a few moments' walk from Kelmscott House. Morris's hand-operated iron Albion press was the Victorian counterpart of the wooden presses used by the early printers listed here.

5 Wilfred Scawen Blunt (1840-1922), former diplomat, poet, anti-imperialist and lover of Morris's wife Jane, possibly from 1885 onwards. His *Love-Lyrics and Songs of Proteus* were issued from the Kelmscott Press in 1892.

6 Bernard Quaritch (1819-1898), bookseller from whom Morris bought books and manuscripts, subsequently publisher of some of the Kelmscott Press volumes.

7 The Kelmscott *Chaucer* is by far the most celebrated of all the volumes from the Press. Richly illustrated by Burne-Jones, it was finally published in June 1896. An advance copy was delivered to Morris, then convalescing in Folkestone, on 24th June. Burne-Jones commented: 'When Morris and I were little chaps at Oxford, if such a book had come out then we should have just gone off our heads, but we have made at the end of our days the very thing we would have made then if we could'.

8 F. J. Furnivall (1825-1910), man of letters and founder of many literary societies, including the New Shakspere Society.

Interview with William Morris,

by Quinbus Flestrin,
Clarion, 19th November 1892, p. 8.

The *Clarion* was launched as a weekly socialist
newspaper by Robert Blatchford (1851-1943) and four
other members of the Manchester Fabian Society in
1891. Its first issue sold an impressive forty thousand
copies. Blatchford edited the *Clarion* and was strongly
influenced by Morris's ideas, as in his book *Merrie
England* (1893). In his first leading article for the new
paper he had announced: 'The essence of this new
journalism; for it *is* a new journalism ... is variety. We
would, therefore, beg our serious friends to remember
that truth may lie under a smile as well as a frown'; and
the interview below is clearly conducted (and written
up) in that spirit. The reporter in this case was Edward
Francis Fay, six feet two inches tall, eighteen stones in
weight, a heavy drinker, and the *Clarion*'s most colourful
journalist.

It was a dull night. Even the electric lights burned
blue. Everybody knew or had heard of William Morris,
yet I couldn't find his residence - Kelmscott House. I was
directed down the Mall. I went down. I found a narrow,
murky passage, as directed. I turned to the left over the
Creek bridge, as per instructions; then turned to the right,

and, after walking briskly for half-an-hour, found myself in the Hammersmith main thoroughfare, closely adjacent to my starting-place. This was not encouraging, but I took heart of grace, plunged into the Mall once more, but this time turned to the right, and in the fulness of time brought up on Hammersmith-bridge. Then I took a seat and moved the previous question.

I remembered that someone had mentioned the river bank, so I tried the bank, and in due course found myself on the Creek bridge again, upon which I counted fifty, recited the doxology backwards, and pushed onwards, ever onwards. At last I found it, a fine old solid substantial brick manse, abutting on what was once the towing path, its windows overlooking the frowning flood. The sullen river and the opposite shore were clothed in the drabness of desolation, made faintly visible by a dyspeptic gas jet. It was not as Morris has sung

> A nameless city in a distant sea,
> White as the changing walls of faërie.[1]

But one could not deny that

> All about were dotted leafy trees –
> The elm for shade, the linden for the bees;
> The noble oak long ready for the steel.[2]

But for all that the scene was unspeakably melancholy. Neither did the Manse appear to me the residence of a Poet. Rather it seemed in its solid substantial British way, to be the residence of some respectable and opulent British merchant, who keeps a cellar of rare old port, and does himself and his guests on Christmas and other holidays. Thus comforted, I rang the bell and entered hopefully.

I was immediately transported to the fifteenth century. Everything was mediæval, and of sensible solidity. No modern gew-gaws or gimcracks here; no veneer or unprofitable ornaments; everything wrought to the highest point of the usefully-artistic. No pretentious shams, no morbid decadent fancy - everything welcome, pleasing, and serviceable. The room was dimly lit by candles, but I could see that a long table by the wall bore a row of old-fashioned plates, and that a broad piece of handsome tapestry, running up the wall and projecting half-way over the ceiling, had the appearance of a throne-canopy. And when Mr. Morris appeared he seemed to me, with his square-set form and wind-blown beard, to strikingly resemble King Olaf,

> As he leaned upon the railing,
> And his ships went sailing, sailing
> Northward unto Drontheim Fiord.[3]

The Poet was rather pressed for time, but he took me into his workroom and we smoked the pipe of peace.

It is here that he designs most of his Art fabrics for his Oxford-street shop. To quote Mr. Morris's words: 'I have tried to produce goods which should be genuine as far as their mere substances are concerned, and should have on that account the primary beauty in them which belongs to naturally-treated natural substances; have tried, for instance, to make woollen substances as woollen as possible, cotton as cotton as possible, and so on; have used only the dyes which are natural and simple, because they produce beauty almost without the intervention of art; all this quite apart from the designs in the stuffs or what not. Except with a small part of the more artistic side of the work, I could not do anything (or at least but little) to give this pleasure to the workmen, because I should have had to change their method of work so utterly that I should have disqualified them from earning their living elsewhere. You see I have got to understand thoroughly the manner of work under which the Art of the Middle Ages was done, and that that is the *only* manner of work which can turn out popular art, only to discover that it is impossible to work in that manner in this profit-grinding Society.'[4]

Furthermore, the Poet, in his anti-shoddy campaign, has been severely injured by the unscrupulous shoddyites, who have actually imitated his true artistic designs and wholesome fabrics in the basest materials. 'It is a shoddy age,' he cried. 'Shoddy is king. From the statesman to the shoe-maker, all is shoddy!'

I concealed my boots under the table, for I was sensible that my last half-crown's worth 'while you wait' had not been an unqualified success.

'Then you do not admire the common-sense John Bull, Mr. Morris?'

'John Bull is a STUPID UNPRACTICAL OAF,' replied the Poet. 'Do you not think so?'

And I had to reply that to the best of my knowledge such a description was, if anything, favourable to the gentleman in question.

Mr. Morris's Poetry and 'Convictions' are too well known to need recapitulation. Still, I came determined to ask him one question, and I asked it.

'What do you think of Manchester, Mr. Morris?'

The Poet started as if he had been stung, drew his pipe from his mouth, blew a gargantuan cloud, and after a pause, as if he were seeking a fitting expression, exclaimed, 'Manchester is a big ———.'

I ventured to observe that, barring the slums, Manchester and environs compared favourably with London, but he would not have it. I pointed out that the population of Manchester and its ten mile radius was not more than one-and-a-quarter millions, whereas London and its ten mile radius numbered six millions, but Mr. Morris would not be convinced. 'Have you ever walked from Manchester to Oldham?' said he. And when I replied that I hadn't, he disabled my judgement, and bade me never to do so. I promised that I would not.

At this juncture Mr. Halliday Sparling[5] entered and informed Mr. Morris that several Israelites were waiting for him in the Discussion Hall, that they had brought an Israelitish poet with them, and that they hoped Mr. Morris would aid them in getting the outcome of the Israelitish muse published.

'By the way,' said I, rising to take my leave, 'I see it was said in the *Daily Chronicle* that you had been offered the Laureateship.'[6]

'The very idea!' he replied. 'As if I could possibly accept it. A PRETTY PICTURE I should cut: a Socialist Court Poet!' And his laugh was good - exceedingly good to hear.

He accompanied me to the garden gate, and there - easy retreat being secured, I spoke that which I had to speak, unburthened myself of that which - to be perfectly frank - was the object of my visit.

'You see, Mr. Morris,' said I, as my eye casually ranged over the dim shadowy vista of the morbid flood, 'you see the other *Clarion* men are very able and excellent persons, but they are very different; they eat nothing, drink less, and cannot say bo to a Gosling.'

The Poet stared in wonder. Of what might this be the prelude?

'Yes,' I continued casually. 'I have to bear the brunt of the eating and the drinking, and the spokesmanship; and it struck me this evening quite casually, as I was walking down the Tottenham Court-road, that if you had any unconsidered Poetic trifle by you, like the "Earthly Paradise," for instance - well, we are writing a Christmas number. Now, your description of Manchester would lend itself to Poetic treatment - '

'Yes, yes,' interrupted the Poet with a twinkle, 'but do you think your Artist could do full justice to the subject?'

'I have my doubts,' I replied, 'and, after all, what would one be amongst so many? At all events; if not for our Xmas, perhaps for our summer Number?'

'Perhaps,' replied the Poet with a smile, 'We shall see.'

Notes

[1] From the Apology to Morris's *The Earthly Paradise*.

[2] From 'The Story of Cupid and Psyche' in *The Earthly Paradise*.

[3] From Henry Wadsworth Longfellow's 'The Saga of King Olaf'.

[4] From a letter by Morris to Emma Lazarus, April 21 1884, reproduced in her 'A Day in Surrey with William Morris', *Century Magazine*, 32 (July 1886), pp.388-97.

[5] Henry Halliday Sparling (1860-1924), Socialist League activist and sub-editor of *Commonweal*. He married May Morris in 1890, worked as Morris's assistant on the Kelmscott Press and later published *The Kelmscott Press and William Morris Master-Craftsman* (1924). I have been unable to identify the 'Israelitish' visitors.

[6] After Tennyson's death in October 1892 James Bryce, on behalf of Prime Minister William Gladstone, had sounded Morris out about becoming Poet Laureate.

Master Printer Morris:
A Visit to the Kelmscott Press,

Daily Chronicle, 22nd February 1893, p. 3.

After its acquisition by Edward Lloyd in 1876, the *Daily Chronicle* had emerged as an important Liberal–Radical morning paper, and this and the following interview, also of 1893, testify to its lively interest in Morris and his activities. Morris's first contact with the *Chronicle* was in October 1892, when he wrote to it to deny that he had been offered the Poet Laureateship. Thereafter he wrote to it regularly, mostly in defence of ancient buildings against the restorers but also, in April 1895, in defence of Epping Forest. His exposition of Kelmscott principles in the interview below attracted a sharp response in the *Daily Chronicle* on 18th March when 'A Master Critic' (possibly Joseph Pennell) launched ferociously into the Master Printer; the attack achieved some currency, being reprinted in two printers' journals in 1893. Walter Crane wrote to the *Daily Chronicle* on 20th March in spirited defence of Morris, and various other correspondents had their say on 22nd and 23rd.

When I called upon Mr. Morris yesterday I was told (says a *Chronicle* interviewer) that he was deep in the mysteries of lunch. So I sat in the square workroom, looking down on the Thames, which is comparatively clean at Hammersmith, and I let my eye wander over the shelf-full upon shelf-full of books. All sorts of books they seemed, most of them perhaps rare, some no doubt of the greatest value. I had to leave the bookshelves and explain myself when with a 'Well, here we are,' Mr. Morris briskly entered. What I wanted was an interview with 'William Morris, master printer' – a chat about the Kelmscott Press, and its mission.

'Ah, I see,' quoth Mr. Morris, bending down to the fire for a light to his very plain pipe. He was, it is needless to say, in a navy-blue suit, and wore a shirt of brighter blue. 'What do you think I can tell you about the Kelmscott Press?'

I told him much, and he bade me ask on.

'Well, to begin with, what was your notion in starting the Kelmscott Press?'

'I wanted to print some nice books. Also I wanted to amuse myself. I think I may say I have done both. Of course, the serious point is the nice books. During the past twenty years printing has improved very considerably in this country. I should imagine that it has improved here more than anywhere else. Thought I to myself, any effort which can still help us in getting the very best printed books can only do good.'

'So for printing, you to-day put England first?'

'There is no doubt about that. Even taking the worst view of English printing, we're far ahead of other countries. Here and there in France nice type may be in use, but not often, and now there are one or two good fruits in Germany. Italy has the worst printing in Europe, and as for American printing it is quite abominable.'

'I suppose you desire to improve the general get-up of books as well as the printing pure and simple.'

'Certainly, the paper, the binding, the whole appearance of the book. Good paper and good binding naturally follow good printing. It would be absurd to waste beautiful type on bad paper bound with bad, or rather, I should say, not the best binding. What I say is, that it is just as cheap to print from a pretty stamp as from an ugly one, and fine paper is not so great a concern when you come to books costing more than 7s. 6d. or half a guinea. To-day we cannot get the same quality in leather binding as our forefathers were able to get, and largely for that reason I bind most of the books that I produce in vellum.'

'Then your object in founding the Kelmscott Press was the missionary one of trying what could be accomplished in beautiful printing?'

'Precisely. In the course of my life I had obtained a good deal of knowledge of type. Particularly I was much among type when I was editor of *Commonweal*. The name "Kelmscott" I got from a jolly old house I go to in the summer on the borders of Oxfordshire and Gloucestershire. It is two years ago last January – yes, that is accurate – since we started work. My prime idea was to go back to that period of printing when type was admittedly the best and at the same time the simplest. Take the Venetian printers of 1470, who in Roman type reached, I might almost say, the perfection of combining beauty and simplicity. One, Nicholas Jensen, comes down to us as a famous printer of the Venetian school. He was a Frenchman, by-the-by. Before his time there had been certain crudities in the Venetian printing. After him Venetian type began to suffer degradation, so much so that by 1490 Venetian printing had fallen off. But to the point. For printing my books I have three founts - one Roman, two Gothic or semi-Gothic.[1] As I consulted the Venetian printers in designing my Roman type, so I consulted the early printers of Mentz or Augsburg in designing my Gothic founts.'

'Now for the literary side of the Kelmscott undertaking. Being able to produce beautiful books, what class of beautiful books did you wish to produce?'

'I thought I should like to see my own writings in the handsomest type, but apart from that I wished to print masterpieces in literature, and particularly to give a turn to early English classics like Caxton's. Take "Reynard the Fox," which I have brought out from the Kelmscott Press, and the "Golden Legend," they are admirable from a literary point of view.[2] Now the "Golden Legend" was last printed in 1527, and until my edition came out at ten guineas, you had, if you wanted a copy to pay something like £200. And if you had gone to a bookseller and asked for a "Golden Legend" he would simply have looked at you as much as to say, "My dear sir, you must wait until you get it." Then "The Recuyell of the Historyes of Troy," a mediæval view of the Greek and Roman mythology, is another very remarkable work.'

'You have been pretty active during the two years the Kelmscott Press has been in existence.'

'We have printed practically thirteen books, although they are not all issued yet. Of these four are my own writings – "The Story of the Glittering Plain," "John Ball," "Guenevere," and "Poems by the Way." "Godfrey of Bouloyne," a history of the first Crusade, is in the press; and so is a quite new work by myself, called "The Well at the World's End." I don't know if it would interest you to be told that "The Well at the World's End" is a romance of the vague mediæval period, and that it will run to about 700 pages.[3] By-and-by I am to print Chaucer, and Lady Wilde's translation of that wonderful story of the German witch-fever by Meinhold, "Sidonia the Sorceress." Mr. Ellis[4] is editing the text of Chaucer for us, and Mr. Burne-Jones is doing sixty illustrations.'

'Are you satisfied with your career as a printer so far, and with the reception your books have obtained?'

'Very much so. I did not expect that I should be able to carry on except at a loss, but up to the present I have made both ends meet. I'm pretty well satisfied that there are a fair number of people in this country who really like beautiful books. I do believe that most of our books are bought, not so much by folks who desire to say they have them, as by those who really wish them for their own sake. I have a small public in America, but not in France as yet.'

'Does the issue of the beautiful Kelmscott volumes have any direct effect on literature, do you think?'

'Primarily the object, I need hardly repeat, is the good

printing of good books; but literature never suffers from being handsomely put out. True, the prices are not the prices which Tom, Dick, and Harry can pay. I wish – I wish indeed that the cost of the books was less, only that is impossible if the printing and the decoration and the paper and the binding are to be what they should be.'

'A last question, and then I shall cease from troubling you, only the question is rather a personal one. Don't you think there is a danger of our losing a poet in the Kelmscott printer – that is, if he becomes too much of a printer?'

'I see what you are driving at. But if a man writes poetry it is a great advantage that he should do other work. His poetry will be better, and he is not tied to making money out of his poetry. I do not believe in a man making money out of poetry – no, I don't believe in it for the sake of the poetry either. You have heard the story of the person who asked what sort of a branch literature was. "Oh," was the reply, "a very good branch to hang yourself on." If I want to write poetry I simply go and do it, and everything else can go to the devil. But it would be a jolly hard fate if one were condemned to do nothing else but write poetry.'

Other things Mr. Morris told me, as, for example, that all the hand-made paper he uses in his books is manufactured in Kent. These things I might set down, but I do not know how to convey the freshness, the charm, and the magnetism which live in the personality and conversation of Master Printer Morris.

Notes

[1] Morris's two 'Gothic or semi-Gothic' types are the 18-point 'Troy' and its smaller 12-point version, the 'Chaucer', which are modelled on typefaces by Peter Schoeffer of Mainz and Gunther Zainer of Augsburg.

[2] Jacobus de Voragine's *The Golden Legend*, a medieval collection of saints' lives, was issued from the Kelmscott Press in three volumes in 1892. The Caxton edition had been published in 1483; Morris had in 1890 purchased a copy of Wynkyn de Worde's reprint of 1527.

[3] *The Well at the World's End* (1896) is the longest and arguably the most impressive of the prose romances that occupied Morris's later years. They created a genre of fantasy fiction of which the works of J.R.R. Tolkien have been the major successor.

[4] F.S. Ellis (1830-1901), bookseller, publisher and personal friend of Morris, took over the joint-tenancy of Kelmscott Manor with him in 1874 and later edited several Kelmscott Press books.

Art, Craft, and Life: A Chat with Mr. William Morris,

Daily Chronicle, 9th October 1893, p. 3.

The opening vignette here of Morris dominating the 1893 Arts and Crafts exhibition is a little ironic, given his decidedly lukewarm response to suggestions to set up such an exhibition society in the later 1880s. However, once the exhibitions were up and running Morris appears to have been re-energised and participated fully with the younger men and women who had been so inspired by him and his work. At the first exhibition in 1888 he had lectured on tapestry, and it is this theme which continues to dominate this interview.

It was in front of his own great tapestry at the Arts and Crafts Exhibition in the New Gallery (writes a member of *The Chronicle* staff) that I found Mr. William Morris.[1] Of the people crowding around this magnificent resurrrection of the art of the fifteenth century a few knew the great craftsman by sight, and even those who had not seen him before felt sure that the curious and old world figure before them was 'somebody.' The flat and very battered soft hat, the worn suit of blue serge, the bright blue shirt, the huge walking-stick, and above all, the round and genial thirteenth–century face – it is clear to most people that anybody who by nature and choice presents this appearance among the smart men and women of a fashionable art show has something inside as well as outside to differentiate him from the rest.

'I don't know what I can tell you about this,' began Mr. Morris modestly; 'the show speaks for itself.'

'Well, since we meet at this point, suppose you tell me something of the origin and methods of what is in front of us. How long is it, for instance, since such a piece of work as this has been produced in England?'

'I believe that the last like this was made in England at Mortlake and bought by Charles I – though you had better verify that point.[2] The Mortlake tapestry production was abolished by Cromwell, but there is a pretty complete set of them at Ford Abbey. You can always tell the Mortlake tapestry by the Cross of St. George on it. There was nothing very original, however, about them, and you would have to go further back to find a true parallel. As for the method, your art-critic was quite right the other day in saying that I used to get up at daylight to puzzle out the tricks of the loom for myself.' And Mr. Morris launched into a technical description of the two kinds of tapestry looms, the 'haute lisse' and the 'basse lisse' (the present work having been produced by the former), the bobbins and 'broches' and 'high warp' and the rest.[3] 'It is, in fact,' he summed up, 'a piece of coloured mosaic, practically ever-lasting.'

'Who made it, and how long did it take, and what did it cost? – that is the kind of thing people would like to know.'

'It occupied three persons – as many as can comfortably sit across the warp – for two years. This is about a third of the whole decoration of Mr D'Arcy's room, and it will cost him altogether about' – and Mr. Morris mentioned a respectable number of pounds – 'but you had better not repeat the figure, because that is a private matter. But it is little enough. The people who made it are boys – at least they're grown up by this time – entirely trained in our own shop. It is really freehand work, remember, not slavishly copying a pattern, like the "basse lisse" method, and they came to us with no knowledge of drawing whatever, and have learnt every single thing they know under our training. And most beautifully they have done it! I don't think you could want a better example than this of the value of apprenticeship. Our superintendant, Mr. Dearle,[4] has of course been closely watching the work all the time, and perhaps he has put in a few bits, like the hands and faces, with his own hands; but with this exception every bit has been done by these boys. We have had no working drawings, we don't believe in doing the same thing twice over. You see Mr. Burne-Jones's drawings hung underneath; they have no colour and no detail. These we have added, subject to his supervision.'

Having got this interesting information and expressed my admiration, I ventured to put a ticklish question. 'Is there never to be any inspiration from modern life?'

'What do you mean! What inspiration could there be from modern life?'

'I mean that to the people who painted the adventures of Sir Galahad seeking and finding the Holy Grail, the story was true. The Grail was a fact; to "achieve the Sancgreall" was the supreme spiritual reality - ('Quite true,' interposed Mr. Morris) - the angels guarding it, and accompanying the knight, were even more than typical. Therefore all this fell naturally and inevitably upon their looms and pages. But to our age it is a fairy-tale - a myth at best; the grail is of most interest from a philological point of view, and Sir Galahad is a "picture-book boy." Why don't you turn your art and your great influence to the production of something that corresponds to our beliefs and our needs as these things did to those of the people for whom they were made?'

'Good gracious!' replied Mr. Morris, 'what is there in modern life for the man who seeks beauty? Nothing - you know it quite well. To begin with, if you want to make beautiful people you've got to drop modern costume. How on earth can you make anything beautiful out of people like these?' – and Mr. Morris waved his hand with a fine gesture of contempt round the circle of men and women gathered in front of his great arras (some of whom were furtively watching him from the corner of their eyes) 'with their stove-pipe hats, their tight coats and cut-throat collars, their wasp-waists, puffed sleeves, and microscopic bonnets falling off their heads behind, their artificially draped skirts and pointed toes?' The retort was most effective, as far as it went.

'Besides, the line of tradition is broken, and you must work in some skin. Here are people with high art interests – what are they to do? "Make a new style," you say? But that takes a thousand years! The Holy Grail people were working in a straight line of tradition – that line is broken; we have nothing like a stream of inspiration to carry us on. The age is ugly – to find anything beautiful we must "look before and after."[5] Of course, if you don't want to make it beautiful, you may deal with modern incident, but you will get a mere statement of fact – that is, science. The present days are non-artistic and scientific – that is at the bottom of the whole question, and we are not to be blamed. For science I haven't a grain of respect. It is not – except in a very few instances – science for science' sake – and that is the only kind of science that's worth a rap, whatever you may say about art. Science is only interesting as showing the frame of mind of the person who devotes himself to it, but "applied science" doesn't interest me in the very least. The Huxley-mathematical sort of thing I look on with the deepest contempt.[6] Besides, it is probably all wrong, and the next generation will look upon us as a pack of ninnies for having believed such rubbish. No, if a man nowadays wants to do anything beautiful he must just choose the epoch which suits him and identify himself with that – he must be a thirteenth-century man, for instance. Though, mind you, it isn't fair to call us copyists, for in all this work here, which you complain of as being deficient of a particle of modern inspiration, there is no slavish imitation. It is all good, new, original work, though in the style of a different time.'

I changed the subject to the present exhibition. 'What is there to say about this year's "Arts and Crafts"?'

'The object of the "Arts and Crafts" is to give people an opportunity of showing what they could do apart from the mere names of firms. No, I don't think we are drifting away from the original intention. The executant generally gets in. It is impossible, besides, to give the name of everybody concerned in the production. A work of art is always a matter of co-operation. After all, the name is not the important matter. If I had my way there should be no names given at all. As for what is novel here, there isn't much, and that's the truth. There is a large quantity of excellent art, but the only thing that is new, strictly speaking, is the rise of the Birmingham school of book-decorators. My own printing, too, is among the novelties. But these young men of the Birmingham School of Art – Mr. Gaskin, Mr. Gere, and Mr. New - have given a new start to the art of book-decorating.'[7] And Mr. Morris walked round the room where his own printing-press is at work turning out his lecture on Gothic Architecture, admiring and descanting on the charming little drawings hung on the walls.

I asked him if he had read Mr. Howells's article in the new *Scribner's*, declaring that no man ought to live by art.[8] 'No,' he replied, 'but with certain limitations that is quite true. Some arts, of course, monopolise a man's energies, and for these therefore he must be paid. Take the painter, for instance. A man cannot be a painter and anything else. Literature is quite different – a man's literature will be all the better for his having some other occupation. A painter, also, is not always drawing his guts into fiddle-strings, like a man producing imaginative literary work or a poet. He has a good lot of hard hand-labour to do. Certainly, of all men a poet ought not to be paid.'

'Who is going to support the artist under your ideal Socialist society?'

'I presume art work will then be done by guilds, and everybody will have leisure to do such as he feels inclined to do. Things like my big tapestry will of course be public property, and will hang in town-halls and such-like places. The community will always be glad to see that people who are producing objects for the public delight do not want for food and clothing. All masterpieces, indeed, should be public property. Why, even in this age we are coming to think hardly of a man who takes exclusive possession of a great work of art and hides it away. Moreover, no man should make a work of art common by staring at it all the time. If I had a beautiful picture I should put curtains over it.'

'Then pending the arrival of the socialistic millennium, the Australian millionaire must take the place of the enlightened community?'

'Yes, I suppose he must. That, by the way, is one advantage of a book. The individual can obtain possession of a beautiful book, and he can put it away and take it out again only when he wishes to enjoy its print and illustrations. Indeed, a book is nowadays perhaps the most satisfactory work of art one can make or have. The best work of art of all to create is a house, which will prove, to my way of thinking, a Gothic house. A book comes next, and between a house and a book a man can do very well.'

'Surely a third ought to be added?'

'What is that?'

'One's own character and life – in Mill's words.'[9]

'That,' said Mr. Morris with decision, 'is metaphor. A character cannot be a work of art. Above all things let us avoid metaphor.'

Notes

[1] The Holy Grail (or San Graal) series of tapestries was commissioned by William Knox D'Arcy, an Australian mining engineer, for Stanmore Hall in Middlesex. 'The Attainment', though the sixth and last in the narrative sequence, was the first to be completed and was exhibited at the 1893 Arts and Crafts exhibition. It is eight feet high and almost twenty-three feet long.

[2] The Mortlake tapestry works were established under the royal patronage of James I in 1619 and employed immigrant Flemish weavers.

[3] The crucial distinction here is between the *haute lisse* or high warp method and the *basse lisse* or horizontal loom. In the latter, the weaver sees the face of the web as he works; in the former, he sits behind the loom and watches the progress of the tapestry by reflection in a mirror. Morris regarded the *haute lisse* or high warp as the only truly artistic approach to tapestry weaving. He returns to this issue in the interview with Aymer Vallance below.

[4] J.H. Dearle (1860-1932) was trained by Morris as a decorative artist and worked his way up through Morris and Co. to become manager of the Merton Abbey works by 1890.

[5] From P.B. Shelley's 'To a Skylark'.

[6] T.H. Huxley (1825-95), biologist and publicist of evolutionary theory, published *Man's Place in Nature* in 1863. In his 'How I Became a Socialist' (1894) Morris evokes a nightmare vision in which 'the pleasure of the eyes was gone from the world, and the place of Homer was to be taken by Huxley'.

[7] Morris's admiration for these young Birmingham book artists was in fact distinctly ambivalent. Though he used Charles Gere's frontispiece to *News from Nowhere*, he rejected drawings by both Gere and Gaskin for other Kelmscott Press volumes.

[8] W.D. Howells had written: 'I do not think any man ought to live by an art. A man's art should be his privilege, when he has proven his fitness to exercise it, and has otherwise earned his daily bread', 'The Man of Letters as Man of Business', *Scribner's Magazine*, vol. 14, issue 4, October 1893, p.429.

[9] John Stuart Mill (1806-73), philosopher and economist. Morris remarks in 'How I Became a Socialist' that reading Mill's anti-socialist articles had, ironically, 'put the finishing touch to my conversion to Socialism'.

A Socialist Poet on Bombs and Anarchism,

by Wat Tyler,

Justice, 27th January 1894, p. 6.

The 'epidemic of bomb throwing' to which Wat Tyler refers in this interview didn't only include the foreign instances which Morris discusses here. For just a couple of weeks later, on 15th February 1894, the French anarchist Martial Bourdin attempted (but failed) to blow up the Royal Observatory in Greenwich Park, fatally injuring himself in the process. This was the incident on which Joseph Conrad based his novel of the anarchistic underworld, *The Secret Agent* (1907). The identity of 'Wat Tyler' is something of a mystery. When the interview was first published in the *Journal of the William Morris Society* Lionel Selwyn suggested that Tyler may actually have been Morris himself. Nicholas Salmon has mooted – though only to dismiss – the possibility that Tyler might be George Bernard Shaw. At any rate, with Morris about to contribute an article on 'Why I am a Communist' to the February 1894 issue of James Tochatti's new anarchist paper, *Liberty*, it may have seemed to him a matter of some urgency to use the columns of the Social Democratic Federation newspaper to make it absolutely clear that he did not support anarchist bombing campaigns.

I found my old friend Morris surrounded by the books and drawings he loves so well, and after the usual civilities I plunged at once into the subject upon which I wished to get his views.

'What do you think,' I asked, 'of the Anarchist outrages; this epidemic of bomb-throwing?'

'Well,' said Morris, handing me a cigarette and filling a well-used briar pipe, 'I have no doubt that you know pretty well what my view is, what the view of any Socialist would be, upon the subject. I regard it as simply a disease - a social disease caused by the evil conditions of society. I cannot regard it in any other light. Of course, as a Socialist I regard the Anarchists - that is, those who believe in Anarchism pure and simple - as being diametrically opposed to us.'

'But do you regard these attempts as the acts of mere criminals or of revolutionists?'

'Well, the acts themselves are criminal. They would be criminal if only for the mere fact that they are a blunder. The effect of them is to disgust people, and to provoke the most deadly reaction. They give justification to a policy of brutal repression from which we Socialists are bound to suffer the most, and they do absolutely no good. Much as I deplore and condemn the acts of men like Vaillant,[1] however, I cannot bring myself to tear a passion into tatters in denunciation of them. But I am opposed altogether to the adoption of insurrectionary methods at the present time.'

'But you are not opposed to insurrectionary methods simply because they are insurrectionary?'

'No, but because they are inexpedient. Here in England, at any rate, it would be simply madness to attempt anything like an insurrection. Whatever may be said of other countries, we have here a body, in our Parliament, at the back of which lies the whole executive power of the nation. What we have to do, it seems to me, is to get control of that body, and then we have that executive power at our back.'

'But you do not condemn this bomb-throwing merely

on the ground that it is insurrectionary and inexpedient?'

'No. Above all, I am opposed to attacking non-combatants. And, moreover, the result of such an act is out of all proportion to any immediate object that the perpetrator can imagine could be achieved, or anything that it is possible to achieve.'

'But it is argued that, admitting, as you admit, that these insurrectionary attempts are but the evidences of a disease, these evidences, these attempts, are likely to quicken the efforts of reformers to eradicate the disease which produces such effects.'

'But this is no more true of the acts of Ravachol[2] and Vaillant, for example, than of any ordinary murder. When a brutal ruffian knocks his wife down and tramples her to death it is generally the result of bad social conditions and indigestion caused by these conditions. I do not think there is anything at all in that argument.'

'Then you do not distinguish between these men and ordinary criminals?'

'I do not say that exactly. Ravachol, it seems to me, was simply a specimen of the *bête humaine*; Vaillant is, I think, quite a different type. He seems to me to be a southerner or Celt, brave and vain-glorious. Prepared to sacrifice his life to gratify his vanity, he is the type of men you meet in all grades, all professions. You and I have met some of them; even among artists and poets they are not unknown; men who would do, in their art, what they knew to be quite wrong and outrageous in order to gain notoriety, rather than work honestly and well and remain in obscurity. But quite apart from the men, the acts themselves are criminal, criminal because inexpedient and stupid, and criminal inasmuch as they are attacks on people who are personally innocent, and are destructive and harmful out of all proportion to any possible good they might produce. Take the affair at Barcelona, for instance; look at the terrible effects of the outrage, and no possible good.[3] Of course the execution of the Tzar was an entirely different thing – there you had simply an act of war.'[4]

'Then, would you say that vanity was the sole motive which prompted Vaillant?'

'All motives are mixed. Doubtless Vaillant believed he was serving his cause by what he did, but I should say he was largely actuated by personal vanity. A brave man, of course. It is absurd to talk about cowards in this connection. A man who risks taking a bomb into a building in that way is certainly not a coward.'

'You do, then, think these are the acts of conscientious Anarchists?'

'Yes, in the main, I should say so. The Anarchists may say these attempts are not Anarchism; but these methods, it seems to me, are a consequence of their ends, and to both I, as a Socialist, am opposed. Anarchism, as a theory, negatives society, and puts man outside it. Now, man is unthinkable outside society. Man cannot live or move outside it. This negation of society is the position taken up by the logical Anarchists, and this leads to the spasmodic insurrectionary methods which they advocate, because you must do something to push your cause: though I admit that Anarchists, in condemning authority, should condemn violence as a means of propaganda. But further, Socialism has made considerable progress in this country – more, I think, than the most sanguine among us could have anticipated ten years ago. It shows that we were rather wiser than we knew – that these ideas were really in the air. At any rate, it is beyond a doubt that these ideas are becoming very popular. And now people having accepted them, to some extent, turn round and say, "Very well, now, what shall we do?" and the Anarchists declare against them doing anything except that which is impossible – revolt. The people will not revolt until every other means have been tried, and, even if they did, they would be mown down to a man by the machine guns and rifles of the soldiery.'

'You think that political means are the only ones available?'

'At the present moment, yes. I think we have to create a party. A party with delegates in the House of Commons which would have complete control over those delegates, and would rapidly grow. The party of reaction would make concession after concession until it was forced over the edge, and then they would probably surrender at discretion. That has been the history of most popular movements in this country. You cannot start with revolt – you must lead up to it, and exhaust other means first. I do not argue that you should abstain from any act merely on the ground that it would precipitate civil war, even though the result of the civil war were problematical, so long as the initial act were justifiable. But with the tremendous powers of modern armies it is essential that everything should be done to legalise revolt. As we have seen, the soldiers will fire upon the people without hesitation so long as there is no doubt about the legality of doing so.[5] Men do not fight well with halters round their necks, and that is what a revolt now would mean. We must try and gain a position to legalise revolt – to, as you have put it, get at the butt end of the machine gun and the rifle, and then force is much less likely to be necessary and much more sure to be successful.'

'The Anarchists, of course, are opposed to all this; moreover, they point to the backsliding of a prominent Socialist in Parliament to give point to their objection to political action.'[6]

'Yes, that is so, but they forget that a party, and the delegates of a party, would be in a very different position from an isolated member, who, after all, was returned simply as an independent member. Moreover, it is for them to show what else it is possible to do. Present circumstances, it seems to me, go to prove the wisdom of the S.D.F. in drawing up that list of palliative measures, that contemporary programme, as one may call it. Mean and paltry as it seemed to me – and does still, as compared with the whole thing, something of the kind is absolutely essential.'

'But our Anarchists will have none of it.'

'No, of course, that is the real Anarchists, who, as I have said, are against society altogether. But then we have the so-called Anarchist-Communists, a term which seems to me a flat contradiction. In so far as they are Communists they must give up their Anarchism.'

'You think they are really not Anarchists at all?'

'They cannot be Anarchists in the true sense of the word. Anarchism is purely destructive, purely negatory. That is why it attracts so many people who are simply rebels, simply discontented or disgusted with things as they are - as they may well be. It is so easy. It is not necessary to learn anything, there is nothing constructive about it. But with the Anarchist-Communist it is different. Really it seems to me that a great part of the difference between them and us is as to the meaning of words, and as to the methods. They are engaged in contesting a form of Socialism which exists only in their own imagination and which no Socialist would dream of advocating. As to this eternal talk of majority rule - it is absolute rot. Majority rule is a natural necessity - we cannot escape from it. If I choose to run my head against a wall I very soon find out which is the majority in power. But majority rule is only harmful where there is conflict of interest. As Socialism would substitute community of interest for conflict of interest, where would any injury arise from majority rule? Take an illustration which I have frequently used, the question of building a bridge.[7] The majority is in favour of building the bridge, but the minority is opposed to it. Well, the majority *will* build the bridge, there is no doubt about that, whatever the minority may say. But how will that injure the minority?'

'But do you think that this will materially affect the movement?'

'I don't know. These people, I take it, are not numerous; and as to their end, they are confessedly in favour of Socialism. It resolves itself into a disagreement as to ways and methods. Therefore they should not be prepared to create or maintain a schism over such differences.'

'Then you do not attach a great deal of importance to this epidemic of Anarchism, and generally you regard the progress of our movement as encouraging?'

'As to the bomb business, I think it is simply a disease, as I have said, to be regretted and deplored, but not to be wondered at. Destructive Anarchism will die of itself when Socialism brings us practical equality. As to the Social-Democratic movement, I think its progress encouraging beyond measure. But this only makes it the more incumbent upon us to pursue a steady definite policy and to form a strong party, with a view to bringing people together and giving them something to do. As to the party; was it true that Shaw said the other day, that there was a party of fifteen already in the House of Commons?[8] If I had been there I should have asked him to name them.'

'Well,' said I, 'Shaw must have his little joke, you know. He must say something original, fire off some "Shawism" or the other, as he terms it, or he would perish. But I did not call to give you my views about Shaw, but to get yours about bombs, and seeing I have accomplished my mission I will say good day,' with which I shook hands with our genial old comrade, thanked him, and departed.[9]

Notes

[1] August Vaillant (1861-94), French anarchist, arrested after throwing a bomb into the Chamber of Deputies in Paris on December 9th 1893. Eighty people were injured in the attack, and Vaillant was guillotined in 1894.

[2] Ravachol (1859-92), French anarchist, tried for murder after a series of bombings and guillotined in 1892.

[3] Anarchist attacks in Barcelona in 1893 included the bombing of a review of troops in September, in which several people died, and the bombing of the Liceo Theatre in November, in which twenty-three people died.

[4] Tsar Alexander II was mortally wounded in 1881 by a bomb thrown by a student member of the revolutionary 'National Will' organisation.

[5] Yorkshire miners were fired on by troops at Featherstone in 1893.

[6] The two socialists John Burns (1858-1943) and James Keir Hardie (1856-1915) were elected to the House of Commons in 1892. Whereas Hardie argued for the formation of a new working-class political party, Burns was content to work closely with the Liberal

Party. Indeed, in 1905 he abandoned the labour movement and joined the Liberals.

[7] The bridge-building example features also in chapter XIV, 'How Matters are Managed', of *News from Nowhere*.

[8] George Bernard Shaw (1856-1950), playwright, critic and Fabian socialist. He was personally close to Morris in the early days of the socialist agitation, romantically involved with May Morris, and author of an influential memoir of Morris, 'William Morris as I Knew Him', in 1936. Of the 'party of fifteen', E.P. Thompson notes: 'The 1892 election had returned Keir Hardie, John Burns, and J. Havelock Wilson, together with eleven Lib.-Labs. Perhaps the fifteenth in Shaw's mind was Michael Davitt, the Irish Land Leaguer, who was later unseated'.

[9] In the 'new series' of *Commonweal*, which had been relaunched under anarchist control in May 1893, the hardliner H. B. Samuels responded aggressively to Morris's views on anarchism as expressed in this interview in an article entitled 'With William Morris on the Bridge of Sighs'.

A Living Wage for Women,

by Sarah A. Tooley,
The Woman's Signal, 19th April 1894, pp. 260-1.

The Woman's Signal ran from 1894 to 1899 and was edited for most of its existence by the well-known feminist Florence Fenwick-Miller. Its first editorial militantly declared that 'The *Woman's Signal* will go into battle. We shall seek to define and defend the place of women in political life; champion the helpless; encourage and develop literary tastes'. In order to do so, it ran, among other features, a series of character sketches of and interviews with eminent contemporary women. The journal also had strong connections with the Temperance movement. The interviewer, Sarah Tooley, was a prolific author. Her publishing career partly follows the feminist lines marked out here, with books on Harriet Beecher Stowe (1891) and the history of nursing (1906), but also evinces a surprising fascination with British royalty, as in her lives of Queen Victoria (1896) and Queen Alexandra (1902) and her book on Royal Palaces (1902).

Journeying from town, direct by road from Hammersmith, I travelled over the ground which Mr. William Morris has made famous in his 'News from Nowhere,' and I must confess that the dream of transformation which he describes seemed impossible of realisation. Where on earth, I queried, are all these houses, shops, and people to be banished, in order that the charming district of Mr. Morris's dream may become possible?

A short turning from the main road of Hammersmith brought me suddenly face to face with old Father Thames and a pretty stretch of country lining the further bank. It all looked so pleasant, gleaming in the sunshine, and was so great and sudden a contrast to the dirty Hammersmith Road, that I began to wonder whether I had not been to sleep, dreamed a dream, and reached the land of 'Nowhere.' A row of old-fashioned, capacious houses, with many windows and innumerable shutters, stand upon the river bank. One of these is Kelmscott House, the abode of William Morris - poet-Socialist, reviver of English art, and the author of 'The Earthly Paradise.' A notice-board by the front gate announced the forthcoming Sunday evening lecture - one of a series upon socialistic topics which is given under Mr. Morris's auspices in the hall adjoining his house.

Upon entering the house, I encountered Mr. Morris himself, a short, thick-set man, dressed in loose navy-blue suit, with a sky-blue shirt well in evidence. He has a bright, ruddy face, twinkling grey eyes, and a large, splendidly-shaped head, covered with a disordered mass of grey, curling locks. He looked alarmingly busy as he led the way to his 'den,' a sunny room upon the ground floor, the windows commanding a full view of the river. Books in plain cases lined the walls; an antique carved oak chest, two or three easy chairs, and a large plain deal table comprised the furniture. There was no carpet upon the floor, no curtains at the windows.

'Mind a pipe, eh?' said Mr. Morris, standing appealingly with a large empty pipe in his hand, and a longing look at his tobacco bag hanging on the wall. The most rabid anti-tobacconist could not have withstood that look. Very soon Mr. Morris was puffing vigorously as he paced backwards and forwards over the boards, and talked in jerky sentences, studiously careful that conversation did not imperil the pleasures of the smoke.

THE LIVING WAGE

'What do you think, Mr. Morris, about a living wage for women?'

'Of course, a woman ought to be adequately paid for her work, the same as a man should, but I am bound to say that in the present state of society it is all but impossible for her to get, even for equal work, the same rate of wages as is paid to men. You will understand that I am speaking only of the industrial classes. In the present non-socialist state of things there are two scales of wages for women employed in the handicrafts or manufactures. One scale is confessedly inadequate for their livelihood, because it is only a part of that earned by the whole family. In many manufacturing districts, husband, wife, and older children are all wage-earners, and employers regard their united earnings as being adequate to the decent support of a home and family. This system results in women being underpaid.

'The other scale of pay to women assumes a living wage, but is, I fear, nearly always, certainly most often, below what would be paid to a male worker. In fact, as a rule, women would not be employed at all in the industrial trades if their wages were not lower than those of males. This means that the necessities of women are used for the purpose of reducing the wages of men, and it has a very serious effect in keeping all wages down. The best remedy at present is trade unionism; let women organise.'

A REFORMED SOCIETY

'How would you bring about a better state of things?'

'In a properly organised society, viz., under a socialist system, opportunity would be given to *all* persons for doing the work most suitable to them. The economical position of women would be the same as that of men; they would take their place in production according to their capacities, whatever these might turn out to be in a state of things so much improved from our present conditions. What we want is to get things on a sound basis; to have the right sort of people to do the right sort of work. We shall not hear then about underpaid female labour. But when women, with their more nervous and less muscular structure, come to compete in the labour market with men, it is inevitable that they must take less pay if they are to be employed at all. I do not say, mind you, that woman is inferior to man, because she isn't; but she certainly is different, therefore her occupation, broadly speaking, should be different.'

'May not the differences be largely the result of habit and training, rather than fundamental?'

'I cannot say, of course, what strength of muscle and strength of limb women may acquire by training, but I fail to see that the physiological differences between the sexes can be done away with. At present it is woman's bodily weakness which cheapens her in the labour market. It is a mistake to suppose that the fine and delicate work of the handicrafts can be done by weak hands; muscular strength is required. Look at my weavers and tapestry makers at the Merton works - strong, burly fellows, yet they can deftly handle the finest thread of silk. It is strength that makes their touch so delicate.'

'And training too, Mr. Morris?'

'Well, yes, strength without training wouldn't be much good, I admit.'

THE PIT-BROW WOMEN

'Of course, I should like to see women liberated from all legal disabilities. I do not wish to shut women out from whatever work they can adequately perform, when competing upon equal terms with men, but I think it a pity for women to do manual labour for which they are manifestly not suited, and so be driven to accept insufficient wages. Now, think of the pit-brow women – you remember there was a deputation of them came to petition Parliament not to forbid their work.[1] Well, I am bound to say that those women would be better tending their homes than doing the hard, rough work of the pit-bank.'

'But, Mr. Morris, many of those women have families to support – often they are widows, and oftener still women with lazy and drunken husbands; they are bound to work, or starve.'

'With bad social conditions one cannot dogmatize on this question; but in the Tyneside colliery district, where the women do not work on the pit-banks, the homes of the working people are better in consequence; the wife and mother gives her whole attention to the home and the children. A splendid set of women they are too, and so are the men. I feel very strongly that a working man's wife is needed in her home, and it is a pity when she has to leave it to compete in the labour market. At home she is doing the work to which she is best suited, and is earning her maintenance if she performs her duties properly. When married women are also industrial workers, they, the weaker sex, have the double burden upon their shoulders of tending the home and helping to earn a living too. This is greatly to be deplored. Our women should not be coarsened and crushed down by this unfair strain; we want to have them healthy and happy, that they may be the mothers of beautiful and intelligent children.'

THE ART OF HOUSEKEEPING

'Do you think, Mr. Morris, that women are only fitted to be housekeepers?'

'By no means; women's talents vary, just the same as those of men. There are many things which women can do equally as well as men, and some a great deal better. I think that people ought to do what they clearly have the ability for doing. I am sure I don't know why women should want to be lawyers; there's too many of that craft already. The medical profession seems to be suited to women; and I am sure women make excellent "men of business" a little stingy, though. Look at French women; what an important part they take in business affairs. Yes, there's no doubt women have a born faculty for business. They can hold their own, too, in the intellectual field, but they do not excel in the arts or in inventive power. You haven't got a female Handel, you know, nor a first-rank woman painter.'

'What about Miss Thompson and Rosa Bonheur?'[2]

'Not up to the high-level mark. I consider,' continued Mr. Morris, 'that a woman's special work - housekeeping - is one of the most difficult and important branches of study. People lift their eyebrows over women mastering the details of the higher mathematics; why, it is infinitely more difficult to learn the details of good housekeeping. Anybody can learn mathematics, but it takes a lot of skill to manage a house well. Don't let the modern woman neglect or despise house-keeping.'

'The advanced woman does not despise housekeeping, Mr. Morris; she only brings brain to it.'

'Good; let her bring brain by all means, and let her cherish the art as her own special domain. Men will never do any good at it. You remember the story of "How the Man Minded the House"? The result of the minding was that, after various tribulations, the man and the family cow balanced each other at the end of a rope, the man hanging half way up the chimney, the cow dangling from the roof. Hard on the cow, wasn't it?[3] Ah, well, I hope the time may soon come when there shall be no question of rivalry between the sexes, and when Hood's song of the shirt shall be a tragedy almost inconceivable to the minds of women.'[4]

A SHORT CATHECHISM

'You are in favour of giving the suffrage to women, I suppose, Mr. Morris?'

'Yes, but not on the property qualification. I go in for adult suffrage, to include both men and women.'

'Should women vote for, and serve upon all local governing bodies?'

'It is most desirable that they should.'

'Ought not university honours to be given to women who - like Miss Fawcett, for example - have earned them?'[5]

'That is but common fairness.'

'What do you think of the two moral codes now in vogue - one for man, another for woman?'

'There can only be one moral law, the same for both sexes; I go in for fair play all round.'

'You think women should speak in public?'

'If the woman has a gift for public speaking, let her "hold forth" by all means. A woman's tongue is reported to be long; but I consider that men are the worse gossips - infinitely worse than women.'

By this time, Mr. Morris looked as if he wondered whether I had taken leave of my senses that I should question him upon such points of common-sense justice; and being assured that he was perfectly 'sound in the faith,' I bade him good morning.

Notes

[1] An attempt was made to outlaw the employment of women on the pitbrow in 1887. Lancashire women travelled down to London to protest against the planned legislation.

[2] Elizabeth Thompson (1846-1933), better known under her married name, Lady Butler, was a painter who specialised in scenes from British military campaigns and battles. Rosa Bonheur (1822-99), a well-known French realist painter, specialised in animal subjects.

[3] The story of 'The Husband Who Was to Mind the House' also features in chapter IX, 'Concerning Love', in *News from Nowhere*.

[4] Thomas Hood's poem, 'The Song of the Shirt', anonymously published in the Christmas issue of *Punch* in 1843, narrates the desperate poverty of a sempstress: 'With fingers weary and worn,/With eyelids heavy and red,/A woman sat, in unwomanly rags,/Plying her needle and thread'.

[5] Philippa Fawcett (1868-1948) achieved brilliant results as a student of mathematics at Newnham College, Cambridge. Cambridge University only finally admitted women to full degree membership in 1948.

The Revival of Tapestry-Weaving: An Interview with Mr. William Morris,

by Aymer Vallance,
Studio, III, July 1894, pp. 99-101.

The *Studio* was an arts periodical edited by Gleeson White. Its main coverage was of arts and crafts, though it also gave space to the traditional 'fine' arts. It was particularly identified with British Art Nouveau, and indeed the cover of its first issue, in April 1893, was by Aubrey Beardsley. The *Studio's* interviewer, Aymer Vallance, had first met Morris in 1883, and in autumn 1894, just a couple of months after conducting this interview with him, he asked Morris for permission to write a fullscale book about his work. Morris announced that 'he did not want it done, either by myself or anybody else so long as he was alive, but that if I would only wait until his death I might do it.' Vallance's *William Morris: His Art, his Writings and his Public Life* accordingly appeared in 1897. The author declared himself particularly pleased with the long chapter on 'Morris and Co., Decorators', which he regarded as the first sustained treatment of this theme to appear in print.

It happened, not long since, that a gentleman from across the water applied to me to present him to Mr.

William Morris, for whom he had conceived a most praiseworthy, if, in a foreigner, an unusual, admiration. My friend had set himself to learn all he could, not only from personal acquaintance, but also from what had been published in this country, concerning Mr. Morris and the artistic movement of which he is the leader. 'I shall get Mr. Morris to say,' he remarked to me beforehand, 'what he considers the best account that has appeared of him and his work.' Knowing well what the issue must be, I warned my friend of the futility of putting the question he proposed. I assured him that Mr. Morris would have to confess to complete ignorance on the subject; that he is a man of absolutely single purpose, who, having a definite end in view and also his own plan of attaining it, is entirely unconscious of what may be written about himself; that, even if he did read it, he would not be influenced in the smallest degree by the advice people might choose to tender him, untouched alike by the world's praise as he is by its censure. 'But surely,' urged my friend, 'no man can be so wholly indifferent to the advancement of his cause as all that. He cannot help looking eagerly for signs of his principles gaining acceptance and his aims becoming appreciated; and therefore he must inform himself as to what the press says about him.' 'Well,' I replied, 'you may regard Mr. Morris, if you please, as altogether phenomenal, but it is indeed as I have told you.' The caution I gave was in vain, though the event proved that I was right. The Frenchman was struck – as who would not be? – with his wonderful personality who has what I have seen somewhere described as 'the finest head in England'; he pronounced him *très aimable* (Mr. Morris had, with his usual courtesy, shown us a number of the valuable old MSS. and early printed books in his collection) but still he could not conceal from me his disappointment at having after all elicited so little information. The truth is that Mr. Morris is before all things a worker, and a very hard worker too. And, unlike many persons who have but little enough grounds for self-estimation, he does not care to talk much of himself or of his own achievements.

When you call you will find him absorbed in work, most probably in the act of designing one of those exquisite borders or initials for the Kelmscott Press; and during the conversation he barely stops working, so that one feels, in spite of his extreme good-nature and his willingness to oblige, quite ashamed at having to disturb him.

'I notice, Mr. Morris, that in the book, published in 1882, of collected addresses in support of the Society for the Protection of Ancient Buildings, you speak of the Art of Tapestry-weaving, at least as regards this country, in the past tense.'[1]

'Quite so; but the lecture to which you refer is by no means a recent one. It must have been as far back as sixteen years past that we, that is Mr. Dearle and myself, began to experiment with tapestry-weaving. At that time the art had ceased to be practised in England.'

'Was not the Windsor tapestry factory then open and at work?'[2]

'Yes; but the method employed there was quite distinct from that which we have revived. For the Windsor tapestry the horizontal loom only was in use, in which case the weaver sees the face of the web as he works; whereas ours is executed, as you may see any day if you go down to the works at Merton Abbey in Surrey, in high warp looms - we have three of them, by-the-by - where the weaver works, sitting at the back and only sees the front of the web by reflection in a mirror. Well, when it occurred to me to revive the art as anciently practised there was not at hand any loom at work which I could take as a model; so I had to pick up the practical details of the craft from an old technical work on the subject, written in French somewhere in the seventeenth century.[3] Our first efforts were confined to floral designs, with the occasional introduction of birds into the composition. The earliest figure subject was the *Goose Girl*, from a cartoon of Mr. Walter Crane's.[4] That was about the year 1881. From that time, except in one instance, the figures have always been designed by Sir Edward Burne-Jones. Our first large work, and perhaps

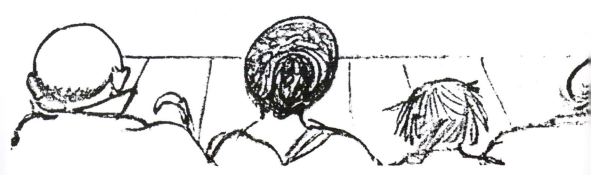

'The Knights of the Round Table summoned to the Quest by the Strange Damsel', the first of the six 'Holy Grail' tapestry panels.
(© British Library)

the best known, was the *Star of Bethlehem*, designed originally for Exeter College, Oxford. We have made a replica for Mr. Wilfred Blunt, and are about to execute the same cartoon for the third time. Our largest and most important work is the series of tapestries for Mr. D'Arcy of Stanmore. The subject is the *Legend of King Arthur*. The pieces vary in width, according to the several spaces they are to occupy on the walls. The height of each of the upper panels is eight feet. Underneath is a band, woven separately, nearly five feet high. It represents deer in a thicket, upon the branches of which hang the shields, with their proper heraldic charges, of the knights of the Round Table. Along the top of this band runs a scroll, with a legend giving a brief explanation of the particular subject which is represented immediately above. We have been engaged on this work for upwards of three years. The tapestry is now finished and placed *in situ*, with the exception of the last three panels, one of which is only just out of the loom, while the two others are in process of weaving and rapidly approaching completion.'

The panel alluded to, as the latest finished, is not one of the largest, yet, in point of beauty, it is second to none of the set. It contains but two figures. In the foreground Sir Lancelot is lying asleep, his back leaning against the stone side of a water cistern, his feet pointing towards the door, shut against him and guarded by an Angel of the Temple of the Holy Grail. The Angel's wings, blue as the

Opposite:
'The Ship', the fifth of the six 'Holy Grail' tapestry panels.
(© British Library)

depths of a sapphire, harmonise with the paler blue of his sleeves, while his white and yellow brocaded coat contrasts with the rich crimson surcoat of the mailed knight, who is encased partly in plate, partly in chain, armour. The execution of the latter needs almost as much technical skill as do human features. However, the difficulty in this instance has been greatly enhanced by the fact that the whole composition is in a subdued tone, with a strong light streaming through the chinks of the door and glinting, where it falls, on the armour and the blades of grass. A masterly reserve together with the utmost delicacy of treatment must have been required to save a scene like this from degenerating into melodrama. Two of the series are here reproduced.

'Of the two examples of tapestry contributed by you to the last Arts and Crafts Exhibition, was not one of coarser make than the other?'

'That is so. You will readily understand that the thicker the wool the fewer the stitches, and therefore the less work there is in a given space. We did at one time try to obtain in coarser tapestries a better finish to the faces, &c., by introducing in those parts more warp threads

103

and a finer wool, but the result was not satisfactory, and we have not renewed the attempt. In the Stanmore tapestries, large as their scale is, the web is moderately fine and of a uniform texture - i.e., the warp threads 16 to the inch, throughout.'

'You are your own dyers, are you not?'

'Yes; our vats are at Merton, and all the wool we use is dyed on the spot.'

'Returning to the subject of the Royal Tapestry works at Windsor, am I right in supposing that they are now closed?'

'I believe so - that is to say, they are no longer turning out tapestries, and the staff is dispersed. Several of them, by the way, are now engaged at Merton, although, as I have already stated, the two systems of weaving are so distinct that it took them some time to acquire the technique of the upright warp process. But the plant still remains at the Windsor works, and the management, so I am given to understand, is ready to receive commissions and to muster its forces for the execution of any orders which may be entrusted to it.'

'Can you account for the success of your own undertaking at Merton, while the factory at Windsor, upheld as it was by the most august patronage, has proved to all intents and purposes a failure?'

'That is not a fair question to ask me. But I will say this much, that they had not the advantage of working from Sir Edward Burne-Jones' designs.'

'Does Sir Edward provide you with full-sized working cartoons?'

'Not exactly, though he goes over all the figure work. The original studies are not above 15 inches high. The figures are grouped and drawn from carefully prepared studies: for the rest there is but little minuteness of detail, and they are only slightly tinted. That is the form in which they come into our hands. We have to have them enlarged by photography, in squares varying in size and number according to the full dimensions required. The enlarged sections are then fitted together, and the whole, now of proper size, submitted, together with a small coloured study, to the artist for his revision and approval; and on these enlargements he does a great deal of work, especially to the heads and hands. The ornamental accessories, the patterns of brocades in the draperies, the flowers and foliage, are left to us, and are drawn, for the most part, by Mr. H. Dearle, who has been associated with me in my work for many years past. Notwithstanding, a considerable latitude in the choice and arrangements of tints in shading, &c., is allowed to the executants themselves, who are in fact, both by nature and training, artists, not merely animated machines.'

'May I take it, Mr. Morris, that you approve of the removal of the South Kensington tapestries to their present position in the large court in place of the casts from the antique?'[5]

'Most certainly. I advocated such a reform years before the appointment of my friend, Dr. Middleton, to the directorship of the Museum. That these magnificent tapestries without rival in this country save for the specimen at St. Mary's Hall, Coventry, should have been placed in a passage where the light was too defective and the space too confined to enable them to be seen properly, was nothing short of a reproach to the nation.'

'I presume you are aware that the change has met with the most determined opposition, and has been the occasion of much controversy in the newspapers and elsewhere?'

'Of course I am. But for what purpose was the Kensington Museum founded and endowed, and still maintained at the public cost?'

'For the improvement of our national industries by the exhibition of representative examples of the best work in the various branches.'

'Exactly; and you can judge by which means those conditions are likely to be best fulfilled. I shall not attempt to bias you by naming which of the two classes of manufactures I consider it to be for the greater service of the nation to develop at the present day, beautiful textiles or classical gods and goddesses.'

Notes

[1] *Lectures on Art: delivered in support of the Society for the Protection of Ancient Buildings* (London: Macmillan & Co., 1882).

[2] The Windsor Tapestry Works was established under Queen Victoria's patronage in 1875.

[3] A volume in the *Arts et Métiers* series published by the Paris Académie des Sciences in the second half of the eighteenth century.

[4] Walter Crane (1845-1915), book illustrator, designer and socialist. Active in the Socialist League and later president of the Arts and Crafts Exhibition Society.

[5] Morris had a close relationship with the South Kensington Museum (now the Victoria and Albert Museum) for many years. Morris's Firm decorated the Green Dining-Room there in 1865-7 and, as Morris goes on to note, his friend, the architect and scholar John Henry Middleton (1846-96), later became Director.

Do People Appreciate the Beautiful? A Chat with Mr. William Morris,

Cassell's Saturday Journal, 9th October 1895, p. 62.

Five years after its first interview with Morris, *Cassell's Saturday Journal* returns for a second bite of the cherry, focussing this time on cultural rather than political issues. This is a low-key 'chat' rather than a formal interview in a 'representative men' series, but Morris himself had a liking for such unstructured genres, once writing a 'Gossip about an Old House on the Upper Thames' (i.e. Kelmscott Manor). The *Cassell's* reporter effectively elicits Morris's views on contemporary architecture, and finds him in gloomier mood about English cultural prospects than in many of the other pieces in this collection.

Upon the wall of an old riverside residence in Hammersmith there is a tablet inscribed: 'The first electric telegraph, eight miles long, was constructed here in 1816 by Sir Francis Ronalds, F.R.S.'

It is in this house that Mr. William Morris - poet, social reformer, master printer, and, to adopt his own description, 'decorative artist' - lives; and it was in his pleasant sunny study, or studio, facing the silver Thames that, as he walked briskly up and down puffing at his pipe, he chatted to a representative of Cassell's Saturday Journal upon the subject indicated above.

'Yes,' said he, 'I am a decorative artist in the widest sense of the term. My leanings are towards the romantic side in art, and my literature is wholly romantic. The Romantic School in art and literature concerns itself with incident or story-telling, and with beauty and ornament, and the loftiest example of romance is, in literature, a great epic, and in art a fine building, properly decorated. The public is grossly ignorant - almost universally - both of literature and of art. It has no eyes for beauty, and it does not care about a story, except for a modern scandal.'

'But is there not a rising appreciation for beauty?'

'By no means; everything is going from bad to worse. You may see that it is so all over the country. Every old cottage still existing is more or less a piece of art; every modern one, from the architectural point of view, a piece of degradation. For instance, in Northamptonshire the beautiful old villages - such as Rothwell, with its magnificent church, which is like a dream - are being entirely spoiled by the erection of red-brick and slate shanties for shoe-makers, built over the back-gardens of the picturesque limestone houses.

'Then, as to furniture, a short time ago comparatively it was of the kind that Cobbett very properly said should be in cottages - good solid English oak and yew;[1] but now you find it an inferior description of the usual lodging-house suites. Mind, I should say that the wealthy classes are every bit as bad in their tastes, and perhaps rather worse; for now and then you do find a workman who would be rather indignant if you were to pull down Westminster Abbey, but the mass of the middle class would not care at all.'

'But surely there has been some improvement in recent years in housing and furnishing?'

'I don't think there has been any real improvement. There has been a feeble imitation, a fashion for what people call an aesthetic dwelling - that is all. People have often said to me: "Cannot one have a well-designed cheap house?" No, you cannot, because the essence of good building is that there should be generosity – a superabundance of material. It may be plain, but it must be good, and if you skimp your material you will ruin your article.

'As to the choice of material. It must follow the country side. You should not build in a stone country a brick house, although with the modern ease of transport we find all materials at command. The village where I spend my holidays is in a stone country, and the people were a century ago obliged to build in stone, but now they use red brick with blue slates. A house cannot look well if it is covered in Welsh slates. They are destructive of everything, and ought never to be seen.

'In London, the ordinary building material should certainly be good bricks, and the large buildings should be of Portland stone, as in all the seventeenth-century buildings; but no stone can be used in the metropolis that is attackable by sulphuric acid. But, apart from the towns, I would ask you to look at the whole country side. Is it not disfigured by the farm buildings being covered with roofs of galvanised iron instead of thatch?'

'As compared with the past, do you not find that in the present age buildings are being erected which will be a credit to the country in future generations?'

'Certainly not, and why? I maintain that the energies of the people are entirely devoted to trade and commerce. Take the very rich people, whose business confines them to the more dismal – the manufacturing – districts. They make no particular efforts to render the places about them more beautiful; in point of fact, they cannot, because everything is a matter of money, and the man who spends his money in making things decent around him thinks he is wasting it. It is a great mistake.

'Of course, we are talking about the great public art – the art of architecture; and let me say that this is essentially an art of co-operation. Unless the workmen themselves have some hand in it – some choice for it – you cannot have a good building. As one of my friends said the other day, "A building is made up of millions of hammer-strokes, chisel-strokes, and movements of the hand."[2] If the hands are misdirected, what must be the result? Because a man sits in his office and makes a design, it does not follow that you get a good building.

'Within the last few years they have rebuilt the north porch of Westminster Abbey, and the work has been done with a great deal of care and at much expense.[3] There are many carved statuary figures in it. I was looking at them only recently. In my opinion all that carving is thrown away. The figures have no effect that is worth anything at all, and there is no quality of art about them. They are simply diagrams. But go to the roughest place that you may find, where the carving was done in the Middle Ages, and you will discover that it always has character, however rude it may be. The man gave you in his work a piece of his mind, and not a mere piece of flat convention.'

As his visitor rose to go – for assistants were beginning to disturb his leisure – Mr. Morris, assuming a somewhat more hopeful tone, added –

'Although I have been speaking in rather a gloomy way of art, I don't suppose it is actually dead – it is only dormant; and I believe that if workmen of this country had opportunities, and if they were allowed to exercise their skill, and were not fettered by commercial conditions, they would still be able to produce fine works of art. No; art schools work from the surface downwards – I want to work from the foundation up; and, in my view, the only way to learn decorative arts is by means of apprenticeship.'

Notes

[1] William Cobbett (1763-1835), early nineteenth-century radical, editor of the *Political Register* from 1802 and author of *Rural Rides* (1821 onwards). Morris was immersing himself in Cobbett's works in August 1883 and on September 4th wrote to his daughter Jenny: 'I have got a lot of W. Cobbet's books; such queer things they are, but with plenty of stuff in them ... One little book called Cottage Economy is very amusing'. *Cottage Economy* was published in 1822 and instructs its readers on such domestic skills as beer and bread making, and keeping pigs, goats and bees.

[2] Possibly Philip Webb (1831-1915), architect and close friend of Morris, for whom he designed Red House.

[3] Morris several times across his career fought against what he regarded as damaging developments to Westminster Abbey. It was in his view, as he put it in a letter to the *Daily News* in January 1889, 'at the beginning of the 16th century ... the most beautiful of Gothic buildings'.

The Kelmscott Press: An Illustrated Interview with Mr. William Morris,

by I. H. I.,
Bookselling, Christmas 1895, pp. 2-10.

After the earlier introductory interviews on the Kelmscott Press Morris is now grilled at length by fellow specialists in the field. The first issue of *Bookselling* was published in January 1895, under the editorship of P. Cockram, and the energetic young secretary of the Kelmscott Press, Sydney Cockerell (1867-1962), had already sent the fledgling journal the 'Announcement List' of books which the Press had in preparation. *Bookselling* published a series of 'Illustrated Interviews', which included such luminaries of the Victorian book world as the publisher T. Fisher Unwin and the Oxford Street bookseller, David Stott. Morris's views on printing and book design were subject to sustained critical scrutiny by John Southward in the February and March 1896 issues. Given the enthusiasm of the *Bookselling* interviewer (identified by Nicholas Salmon in *The William Morris Chronology* as I. H. I. Temple Scott) for all aspects of the Kelmscott venture, however minute, I have had to be unusually selective in footnoting this interview, lest it get overburdened with scholarship.

To obtain the privilege of an interview with Mr. Morris is no easy matter. His time is so fully taken up with his business and his private work that he has hardly an hour to give to what, more often than not, is but the inquisitive prying into the home life of an earnest worker. Our purpose was in no way prompted by this feeling. We were anxious to present to our readers an account of a printing-house of the nineteenth century, where the purity of spirit for the love of the work itself, which characterised the master printers of the fifteenth century, was yet preserved and even glorified by the genius of a modern craftsman, who knew intimately what that spirit aimed at. So that when Mr. Cockerell, the secretary, informed us that Mr. Morris would be pleased to give us a Saturday afternoon, we felt that we must make the most of the opportunity.

Mr. Morris received us in a very hearty fashion, making us at once at home in his work-room, the windows of which look out upon 'the King of rivers,' with the Hammersmith bridge spanning it. We lit up pipes, cigars, and cigarettes, and enjoyed the comfort of an old and well-worn arm chair. To come into Kelmscott House from the hard, prosaic, and matter-of-fact broadway of the "Ammersmith 'Igh,' is to be transplanted from the busy turmoil of a modern suburb to the quiet and cloistered peace of a mediæval country-place. Hardly a sign of luxurious furnishing, except a magnificent collection of rare *incunabula* and finely illuminated manuscripts. And even these cannot be considered 'furniture.' In reality they form Mr. Morris's tools - the helps by which he is enabled to work the designs and carry out the traditions of the artists who made them, and of whom he is himself the modern living descendant.

'And now, Mr. Morris, will you kindly tell us why you started the Kelmscott Press?'

'Oh! Simply because I felt that for the books I loved and cared for there might be attempted a presentation, both as to print and paper, which should be worthy of one's feelings. That is all. The ideas we cherish are worth

Printer's mark designed by Morris for the Kelmscott Press books. (© British Library)

preserving, and I fail to see why a beautiful form should not be given to them, as well as an ugly one. It is just as easy to give the one as the other - only we have had the ugly and not the beautiful. My wish was to show that a book could be produced in beautiful type, on beautiful paper, and bound in beautiful binding, just as easily as we more frequently do the opposite of this.'

'Then you think every book ought to be so produced?'

'Why not? Why should not every book be "a thing of beauty"?[1] It might as well be that as not - and it is just as simple.'

'Would you print, say, *The Pickwick Papers* in your golden type?'

'Certainly. As a matter of fact, I am particularly fond of Dickens, and especially *Pickwick*, and I have always felt that there has not yet been published an edition of Dickens's works in any way worthy of him. I should just be delighted to print him at my press.'

'What, on hand-made paper?'

'Certainly. Why not on hand-made paper as well as on machine-made?'

'Well, for no particular reason, only it might look so incongruous.'

'I fail to see the incongruity. That arises simply from preconceived notions of the right thing, established by a vicious custom. My purpose is, if possible, to change the viciousness of the custom, and make it the rule that it is better to have a pleasing handiwork than a displeasing one, or, at any rate rather than an ugly one. In an age where ugliness is conventional, it is difficult, I know, to appreciate the opposite. The amount of trouble which modern workers take to make the outcome of their effort inartistic is something appalling. The same amount of energy, rightly directed, would long ago have brought about a more life-giving art and a truer spirit of craftsmanship.'

'From what sources have you drawn in designing your various types?'

'From manuscripts and the early printers. Look at this volume,' and Mr. Morris walked towards a book-case by the west wall of the room, and took down a fine old folio printed by Jenson. 'If you will examine carefully the formation of the letters in this book and compare them with what I have called my "golden type," you will see that it is on Jenson that I have drawn for inspiration. The early printers were wonderful fellows for seizing on the main ideas, and they gradually worked out, taking the script letters for their basis, sets of types in Gothic and Roman forms, which we have hardly equalled to-day. Of course we have improved on the Roman letters, and the best work of the Caslons can hardly be excelled.[2] But what I want to point out is that the beauty of the form is with such printers as Jenson, Pannartz, Coburger, and others, almost perfectly realised.[3] My own types hardly differ from theirs in essentials. They are not the same, of course, but they are not altogether original. It would be impossible to attain absolute originality where the sphere of action, so to speak, of the designer is so very limited.'

'Have you heard of the firm in America which calls itself The Jenson Press?'[4]

'Oh, yes, and I have seen some of its work. As a matter of fact, it is not Jenson at all. The same type almost exactly was used by Caslon, and later by the Chiswick Press.[5] On the paper on which the Americans print, with its highly glazed surface, the so-called Jenson type looks absurd.'

'What do you think of the Edinburgh Constables' departure lately?'[6]

'I don't think much of it. The Constables are good printers, but those square capitals with the thick faces, which they use in the headlines of their books are simply hideous. I quite agree with you in calling the type which they frequently use now, a bastard Caslon. In my opinion the best printers in Scotland are the Clarks. They have done some really beautiful work and have done it cheaply.'

'What guides you in the ornamentation of your pages?'

'The subject, of course. In my *Froissart*,[7] for instance, on which I am now very busy, I have made special designs, floriated ones, but having the coats of arms of all the nobles mentioned in the History. You will see from this specimen page what I mean.'

'Speaking of ornamentation of books, what is your opinion of the young school of Birmingham artists?'

'Well, I think they have, in Gaskin and New, two very good men, who have ideas and originality. For the most part, however, they follow too slavishly the opposition to conventionality.'

'We asked the question because it seemed to us that their ornamentation was used without the least attention to the contents of the book. Take, for instance, their book of *Nursery Rhymes* which Mr Baring-Gould edited, and Messrs. Methuen published.[8] Here you have the preface and some pages of notes, both of the most matter-of-fact substance, embellished with borders after a fifteenth century style. It seems stupid.'

'Well, there's certainly something to object to in that; but you must remember that the Birmingham people have not yet found their feet. They will do good work yet, I am sure. In my *Froissart*, and in my *Chaucer*, I have gone to great trouble to make the ornamental borders of the pages in perfect harmony with the subject, and you will find that the same designs, if repeated, are reintroduced because of their suitability.'

'When did you start your press?'

'In April 1891, but I had made many experiments previous to that date. I was urged to the undertaking by my friend, Mr. Emery Walker,[9] to whose help and

HERE BEGINNETH THE TALES OF CANTERBURY AND FIRST THE PROLOGUE THEREOF

WHAT Aprille with his shoures soote
The droghte of March hath perced to the roote,
And bathed every veyne in swich licour,
Of which vertu engendred is the flour;
Whan Zephirus eek with his swete breeth
Inspired hath in every holt and heeth
The tendre croppes, and the yonge sonne
Hath in the Ram his halfe cours yronne,
And smale foweles maken melodye,
That slepen al the nyght with open eye,
So priketh hem nature in hir corages;
Thanne longen folk to goon on pilgrimages,
And palmeres for to seken straunge strondes,
To ferne halwes, kowthe in sondry londes;
And specially, from every shires ende
Of Engelond, to Caunterbury they wende,
The hooly blisful martir for to seke,
That hem hath holpen whan that they were
seeke.

BIFIL that in that seson on a day,
In Southwerk at the Tabard as I lay,
Redy to wenden on my pilgrym-
age
To Caunterbury with ful devout
corage,
At nyght were come into that hostelrye
Wel nyne and twenty in a compaignye,
Of sondry folk, by aventure yfalle
In felaweshipe, and pilgrimes were they alle,
That toward Caunterbury wolden ryde.
The chambres and the stables weren wyde

experience and knowledge I owe a great deal. I may tell you candidly, I was not much of a typographer before Mr. Walker took me in hand, but I have learned a little and I hope to learn more. At any rate I have tried to put into my work the best craft I possess.'

'May we see some of the advanced sheets of your *Chaucer*? The book has been so much talked of that we are curious for a sight of it.'

'With pleasure. In this portfolio I have a set of all the sheets that, so far, have been printed off, and I can tell you the work is a far bigger one than I ever bargained it would be. The fifty or sixty illustrations which Burne-Jones drew originally have grown into eighty, and new borders and head and tail-pieces have also had to be made. You have, no doubt, heard a great deal of the enormous profit I must be making on these books, because of the high prices I ask for them. I can assure you that, if the people who go about talking of my profits were to see my balance-sheet, they would speak quite differently. In this *Chaucer*, in particular, the cost will hardly be covered by the subscriptions, although every copy has been sold. To give you an idea of how easy it is for me to make a loss, I may mention as a case in point my *Beowulf*. It was announced in the prospectus that it would be published at two guineas, but in the printing of the book several sheets got spoiled and had to be reprinted. The mere cost of reprinting these sheets and the expense of the extra paper converted my profit into a loss – and the book is sold at less than it cost me to produce it.'

'We suppose you like the work?'

'Oh! It's jolly fun. I like it immensely. There is so much pleasure in seeing a beautiful form given to your favourite writers and knowing that you have worked of your own self to attain that form.'

'That must be the joy of the artist in seeing the objective realisation of his fancies.'

'If you like to put it that way – yes.'

'Speaking of your *Froissart*, from what text are you printing, and in what form do you intend to issue it?'

'You cannot have a better text than old Berners's. It's fine old English and would take a lot of beating. The edition of the text I am using is the 2 vols. quarto published by Rivington and others in 1812. My reprint is a full folio and will take up two volumes. I also intend to publish it in four parts. Those who may like a strong binding will be able to get one from me for both the *Chaucer* as well as the *Froissart*. It will be in white pigskin - a beautiful material for wearing and showing designs - and the designs will be by Cobden-Sanderson.'[10]

'Who makes your paper?'

'Batchelor, from moulds which I provided.[11] Both he and my binders have worked well under my directions, and I have been able to obtain from them materials and work which I do not think I can better elsewhere. The paper is really of beautiful quality, and the binding is strong.'

'Now as to the future, Mr. Morris - what books would you like to print, and what are you going to print? We want some information about these which has not gone the round of the papers.'

Mr. Morris smiled broadly. He was sitting in his arm-chair smoking his pipe, his fine head lit up by the blaze from the fire. The night had come on while we had been chatting, and the room was filled with the twilight of the fine November evening. Mr. Morris tucked up his trousers, and laying the open palms of his hands upon his knees, began -

'The books I would like to print are the books I love to read and keep. I should be delighted to do the old English ballads - and I will some day. But no book I could do would give me half the pleasure I am getting from the *Froissart*. I am simply revelling in it. It's such a noble and glorious work, and every page as it leaves the press delights me more than I can say. I am taking great pains with it, and doing all I can to realise what I have long wished. I am printing it in my Chaucer type. The edition of *Chaucer* is also a pleasure to me, and Burne-Jones is as much interested in it as I am. Just now I am anxious to put in hand my *Earthly Paradise*. I think it will make a splendid set of volumes, don't you? I am rather exercised as to its *format*, but Cockerell is in favour of this new size – a sort of mild quarto, and yet looking like an octavo. What do you think of it?' We agreed with Mr. Cockerell, and thought the size perfectly unique, and one which would show off to excellent advantage the beautiful borders and ornaments on which Mr. Morris was already hard at work. 'I will issue this in eight volumes, and as cheaply as I can. There will be only 350 copies printed on paper, and six on vellum. I do hope it will meet with the approval of those friends who have supported me hitherto. I can assure you that it requires no little manoeuvring to make my ventures pay, and yet people think I make large profits, because the prices charged are comparatively high. Then, again, there is the Catalogue of my Collection of Woodcut-Books, Early Printed Books and Manuscripts.[12] This will be largely illustrated with facsimiles of the plates and pages of the books themselves. Of course, this is just a little fancy for my own pleasure, and yet I have an idea that there ought to be many book-lovers and art-lovers who would find much in the volume to delight them. Here are some of the specimen pages and blocks. You see that I am sparing no trouble to give the finest illustrations.' We agreed with Mr. Morris that the book would be a valuable help to many a bibliophile and searcher for treasures. Mr. Morris has, perhaps, one of the finest private collections of good specimens of typography and early woodcuts that may be found in the British islands. And they are all preserved intact in the books themselves, which it has been his pride and his pleasure to gather together during his lifetime.

'Now, a book which I am making ready for printing, and in which I shall put all I know, is my *Sigurd*. I don't want to say much about it now, but of all my books, I want to have this one more especially embodied in the most beautiful form I can give it. Burne-Jones will illustrate it, and it will be printed in the Troy type, and on a folio sheet. I am even looking forward myself to seeing it finished.'

'When do you expect to issue Mr. Theodore Watt's Poems?'[13]

'Well,' with a smile, 'as soon after I get the manuscript as possible. I shall be delighted to work on it.'

'How have you found your smaller books go?'

'Excellently well. And I am not surprised. When you come to look at it, and see that you get a book like this' – and Mr. Morris caressed gently the pages of *Child Christopher*[14] – 'for seven and sixpence a volume, it would be impossible to refuse buying it. I love my books, and I love making them, and I think these little octavos quite the most charming things issued from my press.'

'They are all out of print, are they not?'

'Oh! Yes. Quite; but I have on the way a new one – a *Sire Degravaunt*, one of the ancient English metrical romances. It will be uniform with the *Syr Percyvelle*, and will be published at 15s. It will have a woodcut designed by Burne-Jones.'

'What is that noble-looking volume?' we asked, pointing to a splendid quarto bound in the Kelmscott vellum.

'That is my edition of *Jason*. It is printed in the Troy type, and has two woodcuts by Burne-Jones. There have been only 200 copies printed, but the price must have been high (I published it at 5 guineas) because it is one of the very few of my books of which I have some copies left. Still, the price had to be high, on account of the small number printed.'

Mr. Morris allowed us to examine the volume, the pages of which glistened again with the beautiful black type on the choice white paper. We have seen many of Mr. Morris's Kelmscott Press editions, but none to our mind that excelled this for nobility of appearance and beauty of effect. It was almost the first book Mr. Morris wrote, and he has given it now a presentation in book form which shows his own love for his early work.

Time went by without our noticing it. From typography, we wandered on to the books themselves – from books we went to illustrations, and from illustrations

the story of the Glittering Plain or the Land of Living Men

to art, and from art to our personal likings and dislikings. We chatted round the fire in clouds of smoke, before tea, and we resumed the smoke and the talk after tea. The house was ours for the time we spent in it, and we were made to feel that it was so. It was delightful to listen to the jolly gentleman as he sat discoursing of 'all he felt and all he saw,' and while we listened in delighted silence, except for a word now and then to show him that we were appreciating the favour that he was extending to us, we could not help reflecting over the life and the history of this remarkable man – a man whose character is as manysided as his genius is pure, and yet charged with a simplicity as engaging as a child's, and as clear as a limpid brook in summer.

His capacities are so many and so different in themselves, and so important has been the outcome of each, that a just review and estimate of this product would be tantamount to a historical survey of the best artistic and literary influences of the latter half of the nineteenth century. In England and for Englishmen he is poet, designer, socialist, humanitarian, typographer, and artist all in one. The French tapestry weavers and the English lithographers know of Mr. Morris as a designer of the highest order. His tapestries and wall–papers are among the finest of industrial products. In Germany he is known as the 'idle singer of an empty day,' and for his eloquent words and ringing songs for the good time that is to come. In America he is also loved and honoured. Everywhere he is beginning to be appreciated, if not so much for what he has done, then, certainly, for the purity of motive and earnestness of labour by which and with which they were accomplished.

He was born at Walthamstow, in Essex, in 1834. His early education was at Marlborough College; from Marlborough he went up to Oxford, and became a student at Exeter College. It was in 1857, when Morris had reached his twenty-third year, that his first great public work was entered upon. It was nothing less than the execution of several mural paintings upon the walls of the Oxford Union Debating Hall. In this undertaking he had for his associates Holman Hunt, D.G. Rossetti, and Burne-Jones. The paintings were to be of heroic size, and to represent scenes from the Arthurian legends. Morris also came slightly under the influence of the Tractarian Movement,[15] for what this movement was to the religious mind of the day, the Pre-Raphaelite Brotherhood was to the artistic feeling of the same time. Oxford it was which gave birth and nurture to both movements, and when Morris left Oxford he became a pupil of Street, the famous architect.[16] For ten years he studied and worked at his art labours, until in 1867 was established the mercantile house of Morris, Marshall, Faulkner and Co. In the firm were also Madox-Brown and Rossetti, although their names did not appear. The business was founded for the purpose of introducing into domestic art and architecture something of beauty and simplicity. The ugly and, therefore, the malevolent were to be warred against, and although the Company of seven dissolved in 1874, the firm is still carried on, and the purpose of its original founders has been realised in far greater measure than even they in their wildest enthusiasm had hoped.

But it is not so much with Mr. Morris as a worker in the fine arts that we wish here to deal – our purpose is to place before our readers Mr. Morris the craftsman, worker in types and maker of books. In 1888 he already began to show a keen interest in this branch of human labour, for he identified himself eagerly with the first exhibition of the Arts and Crafts Society held in that year. At this exhibition much discussion as to the possibilities of typographical art took place, and Mr. Morris put his views into practical illustration by having printed at the Chiswick Press, and under his own supervision, his delightful romance, *The House of the Wolfings*: this was followed in 1890 by *The Roots of the Mountains*. The type used in each case is altogether different from any type employed up to that date by any of either English or American printers. Since then, however, it has been slavishly imitated by other houses.

Mr. Morris felt that he must now either go the whole

hog or none. The resources of the Chiswick Press were evidently not sufficient to cope with his ideas. He determined, therefore, to raise a press of his own, fashion his own type, and show the world what a beautiful book ought to be like. And who shall say that he has failed? The success, so worthily achieved and so unselfishly kept in the background, has emboldened Mr. Morris to attempt the realisation of even finer work than he has already done, and so he is about to set himself the task of designing a fount of long primer to harmonise with his 'Golden type.' From the bibliography of the Kelmscott Press which we append to this rambling account,[17] our readers may see for themselves that the four years of Mr. Morris's 'press' work have not been spent in vain, and if to these we add those 'in preparation,' we cannot but wonder at the enthusiasm which could inspire so much industry, and the devotion of heart which supplied the impulse to carry it to successful issues.

Among the many interesting and amusing facts which Mr. Morris interspersed in his conversation, there was one of peculiar interest. Mr. Morris had purchased a remarkably fine Book of Hours – a manuscript of the thirteenth century.[18] It was shown to us in all the gorgeousness of its exquisite penmanship and painted initials shining with burnished gold. 'My purchase,' he remarked with a smile, 'was not perfect – it wanted two leaves; but I was perfectly satisfied with it. Some time after I had acquired it, a friend who knew of my manuscript, and who also knew that it wanted two leaves, told me that he had seen framed and hung up in the Fitzwilliam Museum, at Cambridge, the very leaves that were originally in my book. I hastened down to Cambridge, and sure enough, my friend was right. I there and then offered to buy them, but the authorities had no power to sell. Instead of selling me their property, they offered to buy mine, and to this I consented, on condition that I was allowed to keep the perfect work so long as I live. And it is now in my possession, for me to use, but to be given up to the Fitzwilliam Museum on my death. Of course I am

THE LIFE AND DEATH OF JASON.

Book I. Jason having grown up to manhood in the woods, is warned of what his life shall be ❧ ❀

IN THESSALY, BESIDE THE TUMBLING SEA ONCE DWELT A FOLK, MEN CALLED THE MINYAE. FOR, COMING FROM ORCHOMENUS THE OLD, BEARING THEIR WIVES & CHILDREN, BEASTS & GOLD, THROUGH MANY A LEAGUE OF LAND THEY took their way, And stopped at last, where in a sunny bay The green Anaurus cleaves the white sea-sand, And eastward inland doth Mount Pelion stand, Where bears & wolves the centaurs' arrows find; And southward is a gentle sea and kind, Nigh landlocked, peopled with all kinds of fish, And the good land yields all that man can wish. So there they built Iolchos great of girth, That daily waxed till these had left the earth, With many another, and Cretheus the king, Had died, and left his crown and everything responsible for its loss, but it was a pleasure to me to be able to bring together the separated parts. The old boys who worked at these illuminated books must have been wonderful fellows. It seems now as if they could not do anything wrong. Every detail is so perfect, and in such absolute taste.'

'Well, you see, Mr. Morris, they had plenty of time in those days.'

'Yes, but that is not the whole secret. We have all the time there is, but we don't seem to be able to come in any way near them. No! it's not time that is the element here. There is a secret we have not yet discovered. When we shall have found that out, we shall understand our own lives better, I am sure.'

'What are those red morocco books over the mantelshelf, Mr. Morris?'

'Ha! Ha! Those are my manuscripts. I have taken Mr. Quaritch's advice, and have kept them, and had them bound. I used to give them away, but Quaritch said that I ought to keep them, and I suppose he knows.'

'They must be worth something?'

'Oh! I don't know about that. Nobody but myself is interested in them; but now that I have got them in that form, they seem to interest me more.'

We asked and received permission to handle them. They consisted of beautifully bound folio volumes (Mr. Morris always writes on a full folio sheet) of *The Story of the Glittering Plain*, *Love is Enough*, *The Well at the World's End*, the translations of *Virgil* and the *Odyssey*, and the *Child Christopher*.

'Well,' we remarked after we had placed them back on the shelf, 'we should advise you to continue taking Mr. Quaritch's advice. Speaking for ourselves, we had rather have these six books than any six others in the room.'

Mr. Morris smiled. 'I think I'll do as you advise also.'

The bell of the Hammersmith church tolled the quarter after seven, and we felt that we really must make preparations to go. We had arrived at three in the afternoon, and if we didn't move now, it would mean a lodging for the night. We thanked Mr. Morris for his hearty reception and genial hospitality, and we left with a kind invitation to come and see him again.

Out in the open lay the peacefully rolling river, with the reflected starlights on its waters. The quiet of the night had taken hold of everything, and as we walked along the Mall the sweetness and the strength of the man who had just bidden us 'Good-night' seemed to gather power, and we felt that it had indeed been a privilege we had enjoyed. The life of the struggling, toiling, grubbing, and rushing kind was not the life of this man. His was the calm and steady persistence of effort actuated by a pure impulse – an impulse which loves to labour for the labour's sake, and, on that account, knows how necessary it is that often the labourer must stay in his work, and wait – to reflect, to enjoy, to gather strength again, so that the work may receive the truest devotion of the artist's soul.

Mr. Morris is eminently a working man – and because he is that, he is also a thinking man. To the work that is rushed and tortured in haste into a so-called completion – to that work, thought is not needed. It is reeled off as mechanically as one unwinds the cotton-thread from its bobbin. The work that is to be the creator's delight, must demand all the resources of one's being – hands, heart, and head. Only in such wise is labour worthy, and only after such a fashion may the craftsman become an artist also. *Soll das Werk den Meister loben.*[19] Surely the spirit which gives meaning to Schiller's words, must be the same spirit which Mr. Morris feels, and feeling it, reveals his worth and finds his joy in being ever faithful to its wisdom.

Notes

[1] From the first line of John Keats's *Endymion*: 'A thing of beauty is a joy for ever'.

[2] William Caslon (1692-1766), English typographer whose Roman types still relate back to those of the earliest printed books. In the generation after Caslon emerged those new styles of type, later known as 'modern face', which Morris regarded as the degeneration of typography. Morris used Caslon for his own commercially printed works in his later years.

[3] Arnold Pannartz, fifteenth-century printer who introduced printing to Italy in 1464. Anton Koberger, c.1445-1513, German printer and publisher who established the first printing house in Nuremberg in 1470.

[4] The Jenson Press was based in Philadelphia, which had been an early important centre of American book making.

[5] The Chiswick Press was founded in 1810 by Charles Whittingham. His nephew, also named Charles Whittingham, succeeded him in the business and revived the use of Caslon's old-style type in 1844. Morris's connection with the Chiswick Press began early, with his *Oxford and Cambridge Magazine* of 1856, and William Peterson has described him as later having 'to serve what was, in effect, an apprenticeship at the Chiswick Press before he could set up a press of his own'.

[6] The two Edinburgh printing firms discussed here are T. and A. Constable, whose head, Walter Blaikie, was critical of Morris, and R. and R. Clark, whose establishment Morris may have visited.

[7] Despite Morris's enthusiasm for printing Froissart's *Chronicles*, which had been a passion of his since undergraduate days at Oxford, the Kelmscott *Chaucer* took precedence and the Froissart project was abandoned after Morris's death. Only a few specimen pages were ever printed.

[8] Sabine Baring-Gould, ed., *A Book of Nursery Songs and Rhymes* (London: Methuen, 1895).

[9] Emery Walker (1851-1933), process engraver and active socialist, worked closely with Morris on the Kelmscott Press and later set up the Doves Press with Thomas Cobden-Sanderson.

[10] Thomas Cobden-Sanderson (1840-1942), trained as a lawyer, later encouraged to take up bookbinding by Jane Morris.

[11] Joseph Batchelor, whose paper mill at Little Chart, Kent, provided the Kelmscott Press handmade paper.

[12] Morris never completed the proposed Catalogue, but some of the material intended for it later appeared in S. C. Cockerell, ed., *Some German Woodcuts of the Fifteenth Century* (Kelmscott Press, 1898).

[13] Theodore Watts-Dunton (1832-1914), solicitor and man of letters. No Kelmscott edition of his poems ever actually appeared.

[14] Morris's romance, *Child Christopher and Goldilind the Fair*, loosely

based on *Havelock the Dane*, was issued by the Kelmscott Press in September 1895.

[15] Oxford based movement that aimed to restore the High Church traditions of the seventeenth century. It led to a strong Anglo-Catholic revival, with its leading figure, John Henry Newman, becoming a Catholic in 1845.

[16] G.E. Street (1824–81), leading Gothic revival architect. Morris was articled to Street in January 1856, but by the end of that year had abandoned the idea of becoming an architect. He founded the Firm in 1861, not 1867 as asserted in the next sentence.

[17] This bibliography is omitted from this collection.

[18] The Clifford-Grey Book of Hours, for which Morris had paid £430 in July 1894. The friend who spotted that the Fitzwilliam Museum held the two missing leaves was Emery Walker.

[19] 'The work should praise the master'. A line from Friedrich Schiller's 'Das Lied von der Glocke'.

A Visit to William Morris,

by W. Irving Way,

Modern Art (Boston), IV, July 1896, pp. 78-81.

Morris was ambivalent about America. He regarded it as an important market for Morris & Co. products and the Firm therefore took a large stand at the Foreign Fair in Boston in 1883. But he also knew how vicious American capitalism could be in its struggles with its workers, writing to Robert Browning in 1887: 'You probably know how much more violent and brutal such contests are in America than in England, and of how little account human life is held there if it happens to thwart the progress of the dollar'. In January 1896 he turned down Hiram Price Collier's invitation to go to America on grounds of old age, but none the less noted that 'I have always reckoned on a kind reception from the "otherside kindred" if ever I should cross the water'. That 'kind reception' certainly extended to the Kelmscott Press books, which had a major impact in the United States. The Canadian Irving Way had first written in detail about the Press in the American journal, *Inland Printer*, in 1893. He founded the publishing firm Way and Williams in 1895 and his visit to Morris in April of that year combines breathless bibliophilic awe and a sharp eye for a business opportunity. The deal he strikes here resulted in

Rossetti's *Hand and Soul* being the only Kelmscott book to be published in both Britain and the United States. The full story of Kelmscott's impact on American book production is told in Susan Otis Thompson's *American Book Design and William Morris* (second edition, 1996).

From Piccadilly Circus to the foot of Hammersmith Bridge is just an hour - if one catches the bus with the right flag. The Upper Mall is hard-bye, though not easy to find, if one loses his head in the maze. 'You turn to the right at Bridge Court, pass Mall Road, cross over the footbridge, and pass the house where Thomson wrote the "Seasons," next the Dove's Inn, and there you are, you see.' All of which sounds easy enough, if one can identify these landmarks when one sees them. The streets are little more than alleys, the bridge one could almost carry under one's arm, Thomson's house falls beneath one's notice, and The Dove's will just hold a barmaid and a barrel of 'bitter.' No sign marks the Kelmscott Press, the objective point, but after stumbling into two or three doorways, the right one is finally reached, and here Mr. S. C. Cockerell, the secretary of the Press, greets the visitor with a smile, and at once puts him at ease. A quiet, tidy, orderly place it is, but with nothing modern about it. No noise of machinery, escaping steam, or hum of electric motor, distracts one. No mahogany furniture, Axminster rugs, or click of type-writer reminds one of nineteenth century progress. The furniture is plain deal like the floor, and with a 'gray goosequill' the visitor registers his arrival in the guest-book.

No Aldine inscription over the door reminds the visitor that he must discuss business matters only in this mecca of the booklover; yet the evidences of industry on every hand are not conducive to garrulity. Posterity may view Mr. Morris in perspective, as we of today view Aldus Manutius.[1]

It was on the 29th of April, 1895, that I first visited the Kelmscott Press. The last sheets of Mr. Morris' romance, *Child Christopher and Goldilind the Fair*, had just been pulled and were about to go into the bindery. 'You may enter our order for ten copies, Mr. Cockerell;' and it was done 'with pleasure.' This seemed to pave the way to the prime object of my mission, so I ventured to remark that a new departure in a business way had made a trip to England necessary in order to establish some business connections there. My first thought was that Mr. Morris would consent to print a book for us, something that could be issued at a modest price. Now that *Child Christopher* was off the press, and *Chaucer* was progressing satisfactorily, there was a short interim in which Mr. Cockerell thought something small might be undertaken, and indeed Mr. Morris himself had been considering a reprint of Rossetti's *Hand and Soul* among the possibilities. 'Perhaps he would like to do that for you. Would you like to see Mr. Morris and talk it over with him?' Being assured that this would be quite agreeable, Mr. Cockerell said he would step over to Kelmscott House, which looks across the Thames to Castlenau, and if Mr. Morris were disengaged he might like to see me. 'You know we never interrupt him when he is busy.' With Mr. Cockerell's return came the message that 'Mr. Morris would like to see me.' This was an unexpected pleasure. In the master's work room were to be found the same evidences of industry, as in the office of the Press. The large deal table was literally covered with his manuscripts, drawings for new ventures, and incunabuli. Mr. Morris had evidently laid aside his work in order to receive me; and no 'wild and woolly' Westerner ever had a more cordial reception. With the offer of a cigar and a comfortable seat Mr. Morris gave me some account of the work of the Kelmscott Press, and how he came to undertake it. He wanted to make some nice books, but had no thought of developing such a business as has come to the Press. He showed me the sources of his inspiration, some specimens of marvellous old Venetian printing from the Jenson and other presses, all in perfect state of preservation; richly illuminated manuscripts and missals - one dearly loved and long coveted, costing several hundred pounds, had just arrived that day, and as I held the precious treasure in my hand, Mr. Austin Dobson's lines kept running in my head.

> Missal of the Gothic age,
> Missal with the blazoned page,
> Whence, O Missal, hither come,
> From what dim scriptorium?[2]

Many were in their original dresses of stamped pig-skin, yellowed with age, the most durable of all materials used in bookbinding, Mr. Morris thinks. One of his own books printed at the Chiswick Press of Whittingham & Co., and antedating the Kelmscott Press, had also just come in after being for many months in the hands of an artist and illuminator named Reuter, who had decorated its margins with glorious compositions in gold and colors in imitation of the Gothic age.[3] This book was offered to me at cost, about 105 pounds, as Mr. Morris had given the work to Mr. Reuter in order that he might be induced to remain in England. But such work is expensive, and, as I afterwards learned from Mr. Reuter himself, just as he was departing for his home in Geneva, there is not enough of it to do in England to support a first-class artist. But with these distractions pressing upon me I did not forget my mission, and in time I hinted something of *Hand and Soul*, and Mr. Cockerell coming to my assistance, the matter was quickly arranged. I must see Messrs. Ellis and Elvey and ask them to waive copyright, which they did most cheerfully, Mr. Morris would draw a special title, print the book in Golden type, black and red, make it uniform in size with the King Florus Series, and bind in full vellum. All these details would be carefully considered and a price submitted for consideration on my return to America. There was never any question about the price. Do I think Mr. Morris made any money by the transaction? I know he barely covered expenses. The Kelmscott Press is not a money-making venture. Consider the care with which every detail is produced. Mr. Morris does all the designing – the paper is especially made, and costly, the inks are the best that money can buy in a country where vicious chemicals are unknown, the type is set by hand, the sheets are dampened with the greatest care, the type is inked by a hand roller, not 'dabbed,' but thoroughly inked, and the presswork, all by hand, is as carefully done as if each impression were from an engraved or etched plate. I saw many sheets of the *Chaucer*, some with the beautiful compositions of Sir Edward Burne-Jones, pulled from the press, and I do not see how Mr. Morris can hope to make a dollar out of this publication.

Mr. G. W. Smalley, in one of his letters to the *Tribune*, in December 1894, referred to the productions of the Kelmscott Press as possessing certain characteristics, among others 'a dearness which I am almost inclined to call impudent. The profits of one book are said to approach $50,000.' Hyperbole and 'are saids' too often, alas! characterize the public utterances of Mr. Smalley.

On my second visit I found Mr. Morris with staff in hand, and one of his daughters attending him, just starting out for a morning walk. Mrs. Morris, whose health is delicate, no longer accompanies her husband on his 'constitutionals.' The secretary having offered to show me through the lower part of Kelmscott House, I asked if I might see the Rossetti portraits of Mrs. Morris and her two daughters, and these we found in the dining room, whose walls were otherwise literally covered with rich old tapestries. Old bronzes were also in profusion. On a side table was a pot of snake's-heads, a purple flower polka-dotted with white, much used by Mr. Morris in his decorations. But it were, perhaps, impertinent to describe too minutely the character of the furniture and finishings, at this time, or to anticipate the catalogue of the treasures of Kelmscott House Mr. Morris is now preparing for publication, which is to be annotated, and embellished with facsimiles from his books and manuscripts. This catalogue is to be printed at Kelmscott Press, and next to the *Chaucer* must prove one of its most interesting productions.

Notes

[1] Aldus Manutius (1449-1515), grammarian and humanist, founded a printing house in Venice in 1493. A notice above the entrance to it warned visitors to be brief.

[2] From 'To a Missal of the Thirteenth Century' by Austin Dobson (1840-1921), poet and man of letters.

[3] Edmond G. Reuter, Swiss artist, whom Morris had commissioned to ornament a copy of *The Roots of the Mountains*. Reuter returned to Geneva in 1895.

Nicholas Salmon on William Morris: A Bibliography

Thesis:
'William Morris: The Political Vision, 1883-1890' (University of Reading, 1992)

Books:
The William Morris Chronology, by Nicholas Salmon with Derek Baker (Bristol: Thoemmes Press, 1996)
William Morris, *Political Writings: Contributions to Justice and* Commonweal, *1883-1890*, edited and introduced by Nicholas Salmon (London: Thoemmes Press, 1994)
William Morris, *Journalism: Contributions to* Commonweal, *1885-1890*, edited and introduced by Nicholas Salmon (London: Thoemmes Press, 1996)
William Morris on History, edited by Nicholas Salmon (Sheffield Academic Press, 1996)

Chapters and Articles:
'Mr. Olaf Entertains; or William Morris's Forgotten Dialogues', *Journal of the William Morris Society*, vol. IX, no. 4, Spring 1992, 15-24
'The Revision of *A Dream of John Ball*', *Journal of the William Morris Society*, vol. X, no. 2, Spring 1993, 15-17

'Topical Realism in *The Tables Turned'*, *Journal of the William Morris Society*, vol. XI, no. 2, Spring 1995, 11-19

'The Political Activist', in *William Morris*, edited by Linda Parry (London: Philip Wilson, 1996), 58-71

'William Morris, Hero of the Socialist Movement', in *William Morris, A Celebration of World Citizenship (1896-1996), Actas Do Coloquio Realizado na Universidade do Minho (15 e 16 Abril de 1996)*, edited by Hélio Osvaldo Alves (Braga, Portugal: University of Minho, 1996), 31-60.

'The Serialisation of *The Pilgrims of Hope'*, *Journal of the William Morris Society*, vol. XII, no. 2, Spring 1997, 14-25

'MacDonald, Morris and the "Retreat"', *Journal of the William Morris Society*, vol. XII, no. 3, Autumn 1997, 5-10

'Morris & Co. in Manchester' (co-authored with David Taylor), *Journal of the William Morris Society*, vol. XII, no. 3, Autumn 1997, 17-19

'William Morris, Hero of the Socialist Movement', *Bulletin of the Marx Memorial Library*, no. 128, Winter 1997 - Spring 1998, 2-19

'The Unmanageable Playgoer: Morris and the Victorian Theatre', *Journal of the William Morris Society*, vol. XII, no. 4, Spring 1998, 29-35

'A Friendship from Heaven: Burne-Jones and William Morris', *Journal of the William Morris Society*, vol. XIII, no. 1, Autumn 1998, 3-13

'"The Down-Trodden Radical": William Morris's Pre-Socialist Ideology', *Journal of the William Morris Society*, vol. XIII, no. 3, Autumn 1999, 26-43

'William Morris the Socialist Reviewer', *Journal of the William Morris Society*, vol. XIII, no. 4, Spring 2000, 57-63

'A Reassessment of *A Dream of John Ball'*, *Journal of the William Morris Society*, vol. XIV, no. 2, Spring 2001, 29-38

'A Study in Victorian Historiography: William Morris's Germanic Romances', *Journal of the William Morris Society*, vol. XIV, no. 2, Spring 2001, 59-89

'Catalogue of Articles in the *Journal* (1961-2000)', *Journal of the William Morris Society*, vol. XIV, no. 2, Spring 2001, i-xvi

'The Communist Poet-Laureate: William Morris's *Chants*

for Socialists', *Journal of the William Morris Society*, vol. XIV, no. 3, Winter 2001, 31–40

'"The Battered Looking and Middle-aged Barn-Cock": or "An Old Fable Retold"', *Journal of the William Morris Society*, vol. XIV, no. 3, Winter 2001, 49–51

'William Morris: The Final Socialist Years', *Journal of the William Morris Society*, vol. XIV, no. 4, Summer 2002, 12–24

THE WILLIAM MORRIS SOCIETY

The life, work and ideas of William Morris are as important today as they were in his lifetime. The William Morris Society exists to make them as widely known as possible.

The many-sidedness of Morris and the variety of his activities bring together in the Society those who are interested in him as designer, craftsman, businessman, poet, socialist, or who admire his robust and generous personality, his creative energy and courage. Morris aimed for a state of affairs in which all might enjoy the potential richness of human life. His thought on how we might live, on creative work, leisure and machinery, on ecology and conservation, on the place of the arts in our lives and their relation to politics, as on much else, remains as challenging now as it was a century ago. He provides a focus for those who deplore the progressive dehumanization of the world and who believe, with him, that the trend is not inevitable.

The Society provides information on topics of interest to its members and arranges lectures, visits, exhibitions, and other events. It encourages the reprinting of his works and the continued manufacture of his textile and wallpaper designs. It publishes a journal which is free to members and carries articles across the field of Morris scholarship. It also publishes a newsletter giving details of its programme, new publications and other matters of interest concerning Morris and his circle. Members are invited to contribute items both to the journal and to the newsletter. The William Morris Society has a world-wide membership and offers the chance to make contact with fellow Morrisians both in Britain and abroad.

Regular events include a Kelmscott Lecture, a birthday party held in March, and visits to exhibitions and such places as the William Morris Gallery, Red House, Kelmscott Manor and Standen. These visits, our tours and our short residential study courses, enable members living abroad or outside London to participate in the Society's activities. The Society also has local groups in various parts of Britain and affiliated Societies in the USA and Canada.

For further details, write to:
The Hon. Membership Secretary, Kelmscott House, 26 Upper Mall, Hammersmith, London W6 9TA